Lessons From My Brother Zig

By

Floyd Wickman

and

Mary H. Johnson

MGM Publishing
3074 Deer Creek Court
Ann Arbor, Michigan 48105

Printed in the United States of America
First Edition, 2013

ISBN 978-0-615-85629-2

www.floydwickman.com

To my big brother Zig

This book was lovingly written over a four-year period during which Zig and I had several visits. He was well aware of our progress and championed its completion. It had been my hope to present the first copy to him. Sadly, the final proofing was completed during the week of his death on November 28, 2012.

In true Ziglar style, my friend, Rick Haase wrote on Facebook: "Zig is at the top. We'll see him when we get there." The cover depicts the "Z" that his daughter, Julie, saw in the clouds after his death.

Floyd

Forward

An audience of one

My heart was racing.

Somehow a simple dinner had become one of my life's most important events. I was on my way to share a meal with a man I've known for 35 years, but I was as nervous as a circus lion tamer on his first day on the job. My fingers fumbled buttons as I dressed in preparation. A man, his mentor, and the mentor's wife; just the three of us about to sit down for dinner. Where did this fear come from? What would we talk about? What if I didn't measure up to his expectations? At the same time, there was a part of me that held the excitement of a child running down the stairs on Christmas morning – not knowing what to expect, but confident that whatever was under the tree would be wonderful.

This day marked the culmination of a quest I began over forty years ago. A quest to be more than just a protégé, more than just a student, more than just one of the millions seated in an audience to spend an hour watching and listening to this famous "motivator to the masses". Having dinner together was an indication that I was becoming his friend; that our connection was deepening.

I remembered back to the start of our relationship, over 35 years ago. Knowing he was coming to my hometown of Detroit, I had set a goal to meet – one-on-one – this man so many admired. Using every bit of my selling skills, I negotiated a deal with his promoter that if I personally sold 100% of our company's salespeople a ticket to his event, I could have dinner with the great man himself. Falling short by five, we settled on breakfast at the Pontchartrain Hotel. It was that meeting that began a unique and incredible journey that shaped my business and my life. That was the day I met Zig Ziglar one-on-one for the first time.

His passion about solving America's drug problem arose frequently in his speeches and on his recordings. I expressed my gratitude for that, and revealed that my brother, Kenneth, had been addicted to heroin and had been murdered while in his 20's by a heroin addict. It wasn't something I'd told many people, but that morning it came out, and sparked a connection between us.

I pulled a paper from my pocket to share with Zig. Several months earlier I had attended a speech by one of the great sales and motivational speakers of the day, J. Douglas Edwards. Though there were 2300 people in his audience, when Edwards said, "One of you has greatness within you" I knew he was talking directly to me. By the next afternoon, I'd typed out my five-year goal and had begun to carry it everywhere I went. I placed this paper in Zig's hands at breakfast. It said, "I will speak before an audience of 2300 people by April 16, 1979". Then I asked him for his advice.

He reached for a copy of his latest book, and autographed it on the spot with this message:

Floyd,

You're a winner.

Keep it up.

Zig Ziglar

John 15: 5 - 7

I had received the first of sixteen one-on-one lessons from Zig. But what was the lesson? Was it "you're a winner"? Was it "be persistent"? Or "read the Bible"?

As time passed, I began to understand that the lessons don't always reveal themselves immediately. From the start, I wrote down every one of them along with many examples and humor stories, and every bit of wisdom Zig Ziglar ever shared with me.

Those one-on-one conversations deepened our relationship. We've written letters to one another and Zig has provided testimonials for several of my books and training programs. On dozens of occasions he's given me advice about speaking, training, writing, and even life itself. He always believed in me, and ultimately taught me to live the life of a Christian.

Over the years there have been a number of times that I said, "I hope you don't mind, I kind of think of you as my big brother." To which he has always chuckled and replied graciously, "Well, that's kind of flattering." As professional speakers, we've shared the same platform; and I've never spoken without passing on to my audience some Zig philosophy, frequently referring to it as a lesson I learned from "my brother, Zig."

Yet, we never became buddies. We have never golfed, vacationed, or even socialized together. He has shown me how to build a life most folks can only dream about, and how to pull it back together when you think you can't. He is, quite simply, the man I have always strived to become.

No wonder I was feeling nervous. I was going to have dinner with Jean and Zig Ziglar. And though I didn't know it, I was about to receive one of the most important lessons of all.

Dinner

The ride to dinner didn't settle my nerves a bit. While the limo made good time at first, the Dallas traffic was a line of blinking red brake lights stretching for miles. That gave me plenty of time to nurse my fears – that I might say the wrong thing, talk too much (or not enough), spill coffee on the tablecloth, or somehow insult or embarrass the man I held in such high regard. My mind circled again and again around all the ways this evening could turn into a disaster. And, it looked like I'd be late!

Driving up to the entrance was like pulling up to a five star resort. In 2007, Zig suffered a head injury that motivated the Ziglars to simplify their lives. I knew they now lived in a home care facility, yet it was unlike any I'd ever seen before. Standing in the lobby, I was surrounded by translucent marble, gleaming wood paneling, and original art in elegant frames. And there, sitting together, were Zig and Jean...waiting for me!

They greeted me warmly and we moved to a luxurious dining room filled with cheerful "seasoned citizens". I quickly discovered the reason for the smiles and the overall atmosphere of happiness: it was Jean and Zig themselves. Each table we passed held a circle of beaming faces and cheerful welcomes upon which Zig bestowed his wit and charm. Beside him, Jean graced everyone with her beautiful smile and kind words. There was so much love in the room that I felt like I was at a Ziglar family gathering. As we settled into a quiet corner, I took a moment to reflect, and thought, "Here I am, Floyd Wickman, a ninth grade drop-out from the east side of Detroit, sitting at the dinner table with my idol, my mentor, Zig. Wow!"

He began the conversation as he usually does: with a question. He said, "Well, Floyd, how many books have you authored?"

"Seven", I replied.

Zig said, "I would encourage you to write your next book. It is the surest and purest way to leave our message and our legacy." My first thought was "What do I write about?" I already had books on mentoring, sales, self-help, and leadership...and then the clouds parted, the light shone down, and I knew I had to share a powerful message with people struggling with hope, with motivation, and with life in general – the lessons I lived that brought me success. Lessons from my brother, Zig.

Zig Ziglar has been giving me one-on-one words of advice for more than three decades. They were usually one or two lines, and I've always considered them to be lessons, lessons from my brother, Zig. Over the years, I noticed they always began with the words, "Floyd, what I would encourage you to do is...." and the advice was consistently a response to a problem I was looking to solve, a goal I hoped to achieve, a situation I was trying to understand or the answer to a question. I asked Zig once what I'd done to deserve all the extra time, advice and attention he'd given to me. He replied, "I love helping people. Some people I help, I hear <u>from</u>. Some I hear <u>of</u>. Some I never hear <u>from</u> or <u>of</u>. But with you, I've always heard both <u>from</u> you and <u>of</u> you. And it always encourages me to want to help you more!"

I applied and reported back to Zig every lesson he ever gave me, whether it was for my personal, professional or spiritual life. In doing so, I have enjoyed prosperity, deep and fulfilling relationships, and peace. I continue to feel a sense of purpose and energy. I am convinced that Zig was sent to me by God – not only for my own benefit, but to work change in the lives I touch through my profession of public speaking. As I've shared these one-on-one lessons with my audiences, I've seen the magic they deliver. They will work that magic in your life, too. And so, because Zig Ziglar strongly "encouraged" me to, I have written this book for you.

A new quest

There are two things I know how to do as well as anyone. First, I know how to come back from failure. I've done it in every decade of my life. Second, because of those failures, I've been able to help others who struggle in their lives, in their careers and with their relationships. I've learned that these lessons, along with my own experiences, can help anyone live a better life.

This book is my response to Zig's challenge. I hope it will make a permanent difference in your life and in your relationships. Join forces with me to achieve and then maintain the successes you so richly deserve.

Chapter One

The Foundation Of Success

The Tsunami

Tom O'Brien was walking on the beach when a tsunami hit Indonesia in 2004. He was 6'4" and a large, strong man who enjoyed mountain climbing and scuba diving. He was strolling along with his two-year-old son and his brother-in-law. As the water came toward the shore, they ran inland hard and fast. The brother-in-law was swept to the top of a palm tree where he battled the water and wind holding on for his life. The child was somehow placed on a high windowsill, and also survived the incident. Tom drowned.

Sometimes it doesn't matter how strong you are, how prepared you are, or how hard you try. When a tsunami comes along, there's no controlling the outcome. Its unexpected occurrence doesn't allow time for preparation. Even those who thought they were prepared may find they underestimated its power for devastation.

The economic tsunami that hit North America swept the feet out from under millions of people, including many who thought they were "market-proof." Some may argue that those who overspent, overleveraged or were lazy got exactly what they deserved. But what of the others that "did everything right" and still lost their footing? Whether it was the security of a now-defunct pension fund, the retirement plan that was diversified yet devastated as both the stock market and real estate market tumbled, or the widespread outsourcing and downsizing that eliminated jobs once thought to be secure, there were those who planned, worked hard, and prepared...and still drowned.

Such were the economic conditions when I had my first opportunity to speak to the men's group at my church. Preparing, I thought about those who would be in my audience – many of whom had lost their jobs, lost the equity they'd built in their homes, or postponed their retirement plans. Some were facing even more adversities ahead. How could my message move them to believe in themselves again? How could I make a difference in their lives?

I decided to check with my Big Brother Zig. Before long, we were discussing the Michigan economy and its unemployment rate, which was approaching an all-time high. As always, he had a lesson for me.

"When adversity strikes, you have two choices: to "react" or to "respond."

I remember feeling confused when he said this. I thought reacting and responding were the same thing. The dictionary even uses one to define the other, so how could they be opposite choices? But Zig patiently explained the difference. He said that we always have two choices when adversity comes along. We can "react" negatively, suffering the consequences of the adversity. Or we can choose to "respond" positively, turning the negatives into benefits, or as they say, "make lemons into lemonade."

Imagine you are in a boxing ring. You face your opponent. You get hit hard and are knocked down to the mat. You "react" by falling. When you get back up to keep fighting, you have moved past the reaction. Now, you are choosing to "respond."

Every human being encounters changes in their lives that are negative. It is part of being alive. How we perceive those changes, choosing to "react" negatively or to "respond" positively, is completely up to each individual. This is free will, and it is one of God's gifts to us. We are able to choose what we want to think and believe. Have you been reacting or responding?

The choices we make are often a result of early conditioning. If we were raised from an early age to believe that we can overcome obstacles, then as an adult encountering adversity, we automatically "respond" positively because we believe in ourselves and believe in our ability to shape the outcome of a situation. Conversely, if we were raised to doubt our control over negative occurrences, then it is more difficult (though not impossible) to "respond" because we've never before believed that we could overcome them. Have you developed a life-long habit of "reacting" negatively? If so, the good news is that our belief system is changeable through the power of positive repetitive affirmations.

Over fifty years ago, Dr. Maxwell Maltz taught us that the human brain is an automatic mechanism that we can learn to control. This mechanism reacts to our thoughts, whether they are positive or negative. Maltz went on to say that the subconscious mind controls the conscious mind. When we control our thinking to allow only positive thoughts to flow from the subconscious mind into the conscious mind, we alter our external behavior and beliefs. According to his book, *Psycho-Cybernetics*, the only way to program positive thoughts into the subconscious mind is by overwhelming negative thoughts with positive thoughts. By strictly monitoring our "internal voice" we can catch negative self-talk and replace it with positive affirmation. As you read this, are you aware of what your inner voice is saying?

Increasing your awareness is not as daunting as it may sound. Begin immediately to "listen" to the inner voice. At first, you may catch it saying something negative and realize it's been chattering away for several minutes before you are aware of it. When you hear the negative voice, replace it with a positive message. As you practice this discipline of listening and responding, you will improve your ability to catch negative messages more quickly. Over time, not only will you spend less time saturating your mind with negativity, you'll soon discover your thoughts take on a more positive spin. Before long, you will "hear" the first negative sentence and automatically be able to edit in a positive affirmation with almost no effort. This is a habit worth developing. The more positive our internal dialogue, the more positive results we will see in our external world. Could your external world use an injection of optimism?

Having optimistic thoughts – thinking "positively" – attracts good things into your life. It is appealing to people who will be drawn to you and help you to reach your goals. It is a magnet that pulls good events and situations into your life, as well. So how do you become more optimistic? Get control of your internal voice and consciously use positive affirmations. A positive affirmation is a positive statement, stated in the present tense as though it were true. It is a statement that "affirms." It may not be a true statement, but is always a declaration of that which you wish to be truth. For someone dieting, it may be, "I choose only healthy foods to eat." For one who is unorganized, an affirmation statement might be, "I am neat and in control of my environment." The messages currently being aired by your inner voice were created over time, almost like a "This Is Your Life" sound track playing continuously in your subconscious mind. Your own voice and the voices of significant people from your life are replayed over and over.

Unfortunately, psychologists tell us that more than 70% of our internal sound track is either negative or redundant. Have you ever paid attention to what you are telling yourself? Begin to really listen to the messages your subconscious mind is tuned in to. Positive or negative, their repetitive nature imbues them with tremendous power. They can promote or block healing. They can alleviate or aggravate stress. They can alter relationships. Your thoughts become the reality of your life.

Your view of yourself and your world will change when you learn to edit these messages, replacing negative thoughts with positive ones. Author of *The Power Of Positive Thinking*, Norman Vincent Peale said, "Change your thoughts, and you change your world."

While changing our thoughts is important, it is only part of the solution. The most important factor in overcoming adversity is not how we think about it, but what we do about it. So what is the key to effective change? It is the action we take; and the precursor to action is that we must believe we have what it takes to overcome a negative situation. These beliefs might also be called *awarenesses*.

Awareness

Do you know what an awareness is? It is when you have knowledge of something. When you know that you know. Love is an awareness. You don't need to think about love every minute. It is there between you and your beloved, a part of you, and of how you think. Love is the undercurrent, experienced moment-to-moment, and coloring your world. Awarenesses are deeply held beliefs, cultivated through conditioning, that shape our perceptions and actions, thus impacting the outcome of our entire lives.

What would happen if, whenever you faced adversity, you felt a deep awareness that within yourself was everything you needed to overcome that adversity? How would your choices, attitudes, and relationships be impacted by such an awareness? What if you began to believe that not only could you overcome the adversity, but in the process of doing so, the adversity would evolve into a wonderful blessing that you would actually be grateful to have had?

Helen Edwards is the president of a large, successful real estate company in Texas. She tells her agents that breast cancer was the "best thing that ever happened" to her. She certainly didn't feel that way when she was diagnosed. So what changed? She transformed the way she looks at her life and the way she thinks. By battling cancer, she gained an ability to keep the daily trials of life in perspective.

Visiting Biloxi, Mississippi, in early 2006, Father Daniel Griffith was struck by the attitude of the residents there. Hurricane Katrina had taken almost every material possession from them, yet their faith was steadfast. They had a newfound clarity of perspective regarding suffering and materialism that softened minor annoyances. They counted their experience as a blessing. It is not simply a matter of accepting whatever adversities befall us. It is about choosing a response that builds us into stronger and better human beings.

What if you could develop the same kind of thinking in your world? What if you could convince yourself that you DO have the power to respond? What could you accomplish if you were able to condition your mind to believe in your ability to turn any negative into a powerful positive? I believe that power is within you, right now, waiting for you to discover it. Adversity may bring you to your knees, but you do not have to stay there. You can fight the feeling of defeat. You can resist the temptation to surrender. You begin by growing the awareness that you DO have what it takes to change your life.

Successful people don't experience less adversity. In fact, in many cases, the adversities they encounter are legendary – the destruction of businesses built over decades, the loss of sight or hearing, and even repetitive failure at achieving a goal. So what makes them different from people who are not successful? It is their response to the adversities they face that propels them into the ranks of the successful. Their unflagging belief in themselves and their ideas enables them to overcome tremendous obstacles. For them, and for each of us, how we think characterizes our success or failure.

How we think about obstacles and adversities is not about being logical. Indeed, logic may dictate that you really are in a hopeless situation. Hope is not logical. G. K. Chesterton said,

"Hope means hoping when things are hopeless."

Have you found yourself sliding into depression or hopelessness? When you do, you only have two choices: let it stop you, or turn it into something positive.

All around us are people who have reacted negatively to their adversities. They wallow in misery. They have given up, accepting that their dreams are unattainable. They feel hopeless. They sit and wait for something to happen that will change their circumstances. Meanwhile, they are driven deeper and deeper into depression.

During the last decade clinically diagnosed depression has reached epidemic proportions. The CDC (Center for Disease Control and Prevention) estimates that 9.5% of the adult population in America will suffer from a depressive disorder in a given year. That translates to 19 million people this year that will slide further into hopelessness, struggling to maintain mental health. And how do they react? They medicate or intoxicate. They suffer in despair when, for many, the answer they seek is hidden within. What could happen if they were able to change the way they think?

Certainly, the reasons for depression are both complex and varied. There is no "one fix" solution for everyone. But a change in thinking would make an incredible difference in thousands, and maybe millions, of lives.

Changing the way we think sounds so simple. But it isn't easy. Some of us have spent years practicing the wrong kind of thinking. Others thought positively while things were going well in their lives, but now, faced with a tremendous adversity they are tested as never before. What happens when we fail to respond positively to an adversity? We are stopped in our tracks. We stay stopped for a while, then we begin to slide backward. Our energy level is low; we feel unenthusiastic about the future, and we begin to convince ourselves that the situation is beyond our control   The subconscious mind reviews that negative sound track again and again until hopelessness starts to settle in for a long stay. This state of mind is called a "slump".

So what's the trick to getting out of a slump? Get out quickly. The longer you stay stopped, the more difficult it is to get out, and the less likely it becomes that you will dig out of it. Change begins with the awareness that you are indeed in a slump. From there, you need to move toward improvement. Fortunately, thousands of books have been written to help people improve themselves.

All the books in the world won't change anyone though, unless they begin by developing three awarenesses. They are:

1. *Adversity breeds success*

In order to succeed, we must face adversity and accept that there is no success without struggle. We try so hard to resist this truth, don't we? Instead, our response to the challenges in front of us must change. My friend, Og Mandino, was one of the world's most prolific authors who wrote frequently about success. I have always loved reading his books because he was a straight shooter, yet so profound. His two most famous books are *The Greatest Salesman In The World* and *The Greatest Secret In The World*. He wrote,

"Obstacles are necessary for success, because in selling, victory comes only after many struggles and countless defeats. Yet each struggle, each defeat, sharpens your skills and strengths, your courage and your endurance, your ability and your confidence and thus each obstacle is a comrade in arms forcing you to become better or quit. Each rebuff is an opportunity to move forward.

Turn away from them, avoid them, and you throw away your future."

It is by battling obstacles that we grow stronger. We become who we are by fighting the good fight. One drowns not by falling into the water, but by not getting out! Faced with a complex problem, we tend to look only for complex solutions when in fact the level of difficulty may be all in our minds.

What if we could think that way about the challenges we face? What if we believed the adversity was actually a blessing designed to strengthen us and propel us closer toward our destiny? The actions we take to overcome adversity are a necessary ingredient to succeeding. Adversity always precedes success. Adversity breeds success.

2. The longer I am in a slump, the deeper the hole gets and the harder it is to get out

If we allow it to, adversity can stop us. Sometimes when the answer is not immediately apparent, we settle in to wait it out. Or we blame. Have you ever looked outside yourself to fault someone who could be held responsible for the adversity you were facing? As Zig has always said, "When we point a finger at the cause, there are three times as many fingers pointing back at the real reason." Like anything, the longer we tolerate the intolerable, the more difficult it is to move toward change. The longer you carry around that extra ten pounds, the harder it will be to get rid of. The longer you accept a dirty home environment, the harder you'll have to work to get it clean again.

If you've been in a slump for a while, there's no point in berating yourself about all that you "should have done" before. You cannot change the past. There is only one thing that matters: what you do now. Recognize right now, this very moment, that you are in a slump and that from today forward, the longer you allow yourself to stay there, the harder it will be to get out. Are you ready to get out of that slump yet?

3. *If it is to be, it is up to me*

Ten words, each with only two letters, yet one of the most profound sentences in the English language. For change to happen, this awareness must burrow deep within you and become a part of the very fabric of which you are made. You must accept that no one can do this for you, and that past choices are exactly that: past. There is no magic time machine that will transport you back so that you can make a better decision. What has happened, has happened already. Wallowing in "I'm-powerless-to-change-it" thinking stymies growth. Does that mean it's impossible to change? Of course not. But it is only the future that can be changed, not the past. And to change the future, you cannot look to the external. All change begins within. The solution is within you. If your life is going to change, you are the only one who can do it.

This is the part that holds most people back from the fullness of life, from the joy and the success that they desire. It is an awesome responsibility to accept that the shape of your future is completely up to you, and you alone, isn't it? It means that no one can decide for you. Nor can anyone "make you" do anything. Even if you give to others the power to make those decisions, you remain the one who chose to do that. As my friend Les Brown says, "When you die, there'll only be one in the box." Take responsibility for your life and your future. If is it to be, it is up to me, and only me.

11

You were not created to live a life of mediocrity. You were born with the potential for greatness. Wake yourself up! Once you have opened your mind and heart to accept and develop that gift of greatness with these three awarenesses, there's only one thing that can hold you back: a lack of motivation.

Lack of motivation

Here we are in the land of opportunity, a country no less ripe with opportunity than at its birth, yet there are millions of people lying across the sofa right now who fail to see the opportunities before them. They feel paralyzed by the circumstances of their lives. They see only the reasons that they are failing and nothing of the "silver lining" in their situation. Are you one of them?

Among the reasons so many suffer from a lack of motivation, are:

Fear

Emotion drives what we do or don't do, and fear is one of the most powerful emotions. Uncertainty of the outcome or fear of losing what we have can hold us in place as fiercely as iron bars. For some people, the fear of failing stops them from trying to succeed. For others, it may be the fear of having to do what they have to do to succeed. What fears are holding you in place?

Whatever its root, fear is a powerful dream-stopper that can keep us permanently entrenched in a negative situation.

External influences

Sometimes we allow other people to impact our motivation. When someone we perceive as significant makes a statement about us, we can slide into the trap of believing that statement is an absolute truth. We may even twist the words they use and hear a message they didn't intend. Perhaps you were told you were not smart enough or that you were shy – and you've been living as though it were true ever since. Mr. Holt was the principal at Osborne High School and the third school to agree that I should leave before finishing ninth grade. I'll never forget the day he told my mother, "Mrs. Wickman, your son is a loser. He's never going to amount to anything." Did he really say those exact words? I don't know. Perhaps he said, "If he doesn't change, he'll be a loser." What I heard, and internalized for years afterward, was that I was a loser. That was the message I replayed over and over. It validated all the thoughts I was already having about my ability to succeed.

When we hear negative statements we can allow them to color our self-perception, or we can use them to motivate us to succeed. It took me many years to realize that I could change how I thought about Mr. Holt's statement, and I dedicated my first book to him. He taught me that we can spend too much time worrying about what others might think or say and fearing their disapproval. What statements made by others do you replay in your mind? Have you grown accustomed to believing that those statements are true? Are the messages positive or negative? Negative messages can become external influences that hold us firmly in mediocrity and crush our motivation to succeed.

Internal influences

Negative self-talk can defeat us before we begin. When we tell ourselves we will probably fail, or we "always" have bad judgment, or "it's not in our hands," we become self-stoppers rather than self-starters. Failure to condition our inner voice to speak encouraging words keeps us thinking like a loser, rather than a winner.

Waiting for someone else

The basic premise of Colette Downing's book, *Cinderella Complex*, is that some women fear independence and long for a knight in shining armor to rescue them from the problems and situations they face. Certainly, this is not a gender-specific malady. Both men and women can find themselves in a holding pattern, waiting for someone to rescue them. They may defer to a boss or spouse or parent. They long for someone who will sweep them off their feet and take them to a place with no troubles. What is the likelihood of a gallant rider on a white horse coming to face your issues for you? Minimal; yet the tendency to defer action until someone helps us make decisions is common, and may hold us in place indefinitely.

Not knowing what the first step is

Indecision and lack of direction can stop us in our tracks. If we don't know where we are going, how are we going to get there? Feeling paralyzed can cost us years of misery. How many people do you know that are trapped in jobs they hate, but have completely stopped looking for alternative choices? They've resigned themselves to the fact that they are miserable and no longer invest effort in thinking about the "first step" to making change in their lives happen.

Believe

Turning a negative situation into a positive force in our lives won't happen unless we can get ourselves motivated. Do you have a motivation problem? If so, there are only two methods for dealing with it. One is to keep digging and digging until you reach the root cause of the problem so it can be solved. Simply find a psychologist who will probe into your childhood eating habits or how you were potty trained to discover the reason you are unhappy thirty years later. It is easy to get distracted trying to discover and justify the reason you are "stuck."

The alternative method for fixing your motivation problem is to change your behavior. Is the reason for your lack of motivation even important? No. There is only one thing that matters: that you recognize that it is up to you to get yourself motivated. Fortunately, you are eligible for divine assistance. God doesn't give us the power to overcome before we start. But He gives us that power as we overcome.

So, it begins within you. You begin by believing. You can choose to believe that you have within yourself the power to change your life. Do you believe that? The strength, the divine help, will come AS you proceed. But the motivation to move forward starts with you. First, you must believe that you can change. Then, to overcome adversity, you must act. You must move forward. And to move forward, you must take the first step. You will learn the steps in the next chapter, but before we get there, I have some questions for you.

Are you willing to embrace these lessons and work them into your life?

Will you allow them to lead you to the right awarenesses?

You can use Zig's lessons as a guidepost in your life to evaluate where you are right now and where you want to be in the future. Have you discovered that this book isn't a quick read? Has it already got you thinking about how you are going to determine your future?

If you are still reading with the right intent, you are about to undertake a profound journey that will require objective self-examination. It may be the most important journey of your life. Spend some time in deep thought about how you are now living and how you might allow the greatness that was planted within you to blossom, reconfiguring your thoughts, your life, and your reality. You arrived without an instruction manual, but there is no doubt that you are here for a specific purpose. What is it? Take this opportunity to choose your direction so that your greatness will be realized and you may flourish. If you don't do it now, when will be a better time? Tell yourself now: "If it is to be, it is up to me!"

Chapter Two

The Journey

The first step in any process is the one we fear the most, and often the most difficult part of our journey. For a salesperson, it's the first call. For a skydiver, it's the first jump. For an addict, it's admitting the addiction is out of control. Your reluctance to take that first step may prevent you from becoming the person you were destined to become. Instead, change the way you are thinking about it. Consider the first step to be a part of a dance.

Having grown up in Motown, I have always been interested in dancing. When we were first married we often danced at parties with our friends. We loved to put on our favorite music and watch it pull people out of their seats. One thing I love about dancing is that you don't have to be born with any special abilities. In fact, neither your socioeconomic status nor your academic skills have anything to do with how well you dance. Anyone can look like a pro if they practice the steps often enough. And every dance is made up of steps, isn't it? That is the common denominator of all dancing, whether you prefer to jitterbug or to rumba.

The Dance of Success

Throughout my life, I've faced many types of adversities, and faced them many times. Yet I have been able to bounce back from those confrontations and go on to reach an even higher level of success than before. Thinking of success as a dance, with steps, has helped me to make comebacks all my life. May I teach you the dance of success? It goes like this: three steps forward, two steps back. Then three steps forward, two steps back. Wow! You're dancing!

A word of warning: don't get those steps in the wrong order. If you go two steps forward and three steps back, you won't end up where you want to be! Look around at all the people you know that have spent their whole lives going two steps forward, then three steps back. They have never understood why things don't work out for them, when in truth, they've simply gotten the order of the steps mixed up.

Being a professional speaker, I've often had the opportunity to speak at awards and recognition ceremonies. I always enjoy watching the recipients cross the stage to shake hands with the company president and claim their trophy. The Academy Awards each year offers the same opportunity to all of us. We see the award winner strut across the stage with confidence, and grasp that trophy as though they always knew it was within their reach. But that's not really how they arrived in that spot, is it? They began their journey with a single step. They felt fear, they suffered indecision and self-doubt, but they took the next step anyway. Then the step after that. And just when things were looking like they were going to be okay, what happened? A setback. It may have been an illness, a rejection, a financial loss – but it was a setback just the same.

Success is an elusive mistress. She leads us on, only to vanish from our reach. That is when it is time for two steps back. This is the moment that so many who have been dancing leave for the sidelines. They quit. They begin to see themselves as incapable of succeeding since they are clearly going backward. But when we understand that success is a dance, we don't quit. We are aware of taking those two steps back, but in our minds and our hearts we are reminding ourselves that we are dancing! We are preparing ourselves to move forward again, poised and ready, and light on our feet – watching for the moment, believing it will come. We dance.

Imagine if the next award winner were to receive her trophy the way she earned it. We would chuckle as we watch her stride confidently three steps forward, then stop and take two steps backward. Then she'd move forward again – eager to reach her goal. Except after three broad strides, she'd stop, stepping back twice. Regaining her equilibrium, she would march forward, reach for the award and hold it aloft. All would applaud. You and I would recognize that she was simply emulating the journey she undertook to reach her goal as an example for us.

Have you been taking a step or two backward? Did you think that was a signal that you would go forward no more? Change the way you perceive your position. No one reaches the goal without dancing. So, get ready. You are about to learn the first three steps to the dance.

The First Three Steps

Step One: Set a goal

Step Two: Make a commitment

Step Three: Do the basics

A few years ago, Linda and I were taking one of our annual honeymoons in upstate Michigan. Known as "up north" to Michiganders, the resort was beautiful and restorative. We awoke early and headed for the fitness center. We had the place to ourselves, and soon I was striding alongside Linda on the treadmill, working up quite a sweat.

My wife is my inspiration. Though she was diagnosed with multiple sclerosis fourteen years ago, she works hard to improve her balance and ability to walk without continuous use of a cane. She lifts weights and spends time on the treadmill every day. So there she was next to me, but moving at about a tenth of my speed.

Several days later when we were back home, I realized she was feeling rather sad. She didn't express it aloud, but after 46 years of marriage, I've learned to detect the little signs that indicate the start of a depression. As I gently questioned her, she began to cry. It was then that I realized that she'd not been on the treadmill since the resort. She sobbed, "Why can't I walk? I want to be able to walk, and I can't!"

My heart was breaking. What could I do that would make a difference? I said a quick prayer, asking God to give me the right words to help my beloved wife. I realized that she needed what anyone needs when they are feeling a sense of hopelessness, when they are unsure and doubting. She needed to start dancing. And I knew the most difficult part would be the first step.

Step One

Step One is to <u>set a goal</u>. This is completely different from fantasizing or from making a wish. For a goal to be a goal it has to have certain ingredients. If it doesn't have every one of the right ingredients it's not a goal, and it probably won't ever be realized.

The first ingredient of a goal is that it be specific. You cannot just say, "I want a new car." To be specific, you would need to know exactly what make, model, color interior and color exterior that you want. You would need to choose which features your new car will have. Will it have a built-in navigational system, leather seats with seat warmers, and a dvd player in the back seat? If you cannot see the picture of exactly what you want, it is just a fantasy.

A goal is something that is obtainable. If you happen to be 50 years old with a height of 5' 9" the likelihood you will play basketball at the NBA level is pretty small. No matter how hard you train or how much you desire it, the goal is simply not obtainable. Certainly, there are times when even a true goal may seem like an impossibility, but it must be at least possible to attain for it to be a real goal. Another example of impossibility might be losing 25 pounds in a week. Losing 25 pounds is not impossible, but doing so within a week causes the target to be unobtainable. What are you aiming for? Whatever it is, it must be something that is attainable within the realm of possibility.

Next, a goal must be something you can "see" yourself having. You may be able to imagine the cruise ship, but can you see yourself on the ship? If you cannot, it's just a fantasy.

Finally, a goal has to be something you want for you. It is not something that someone else wants you to want. I have often joked with leadership that I am planning to come out with a new pamphlet called, "How To De-Motivate Your Staff." When you open the pamphlet, there will only be four words inside. It will say, "Give them a goal." Motivation comes from within, not at the request of someone else. If you want to motivate someone, your challenge is to help them to discover what they want and to get specific about it. Then show them how to get it. Has someone been trying to motivate you? No wonder it hasn't been working.

Your goal might be to give something to someone; it doesn't have to be a material item for yourself. You may dream of taking your grandchildren to Disney World or buying a new fishing boat for your husband.   Keep in mind that YOU are the one who has to want it. The boat won't work as a goal if it's something your spouse wants, but you despise fishing and resent his time on the lake. So the gift you are giving is really for yourself. That's what makes it work as a goal. You are offering an experience only you can bring to those you love. What would delight you? What could you do for or give to the important people in your life that would bring you joy? Determining what you want for you creates the kind of motivation that will carry you to the desired destination. If you want to motivate yourself, give yourself a goal that makes you burn with passion.

When a goal is specific, obtainable, visualized, and something that you want, it generates physical energy. Years ago, an article in *The Detroit News* featured a doctor's advice column. A woman, asking for help, said she didn't feel like doing anything. She could hardly get herself to leave the house to shop for groceries. She had no interest in cooking or doing anything but sitting on the sofa and watching television. The first words of the doctor's response were, "Set a goal."

If you need energy, if you have a desire to change your circumstances, if you need purpose in your life, you must set a goal. It is the first step to making the change you desire. And now you know that the goal must be specific, obtainable, visualized, and something you want for you. Have you thought of a goal yet?   Can you feel the excitement of reaching it already?

I was thinking of these ingredients as I started questioning Linda. I began by saying, "Honey, you do have MS. When you say you want to walk, what would make you feel good?" We bounced ideas back and forth until she admitted to me, "If I could walk a mile in 20 minutes, that would be wonderful."

So I clarified, "So right now, you're walking a mile in an hour. If you could just walk a mile in 20 minutes you'd feel like a million bucks, right?" She agreed.

To measure her progress, I drew a picture of a thermometer on a big piece of white poster board. I placed the goal of walking one mile within 20 minutes at the top. She agreed to walk 20 minutes every day, and to strive toward walking faster. We posted the thermometer where we could both see it, and she tracked her progress. In less than 30 days, she hit the goal. Was it because her MS was in remission? Of course not. It was because Linda's attitude about walking had changed completely. She had become confident that she could overcome the obstacles she faced. That's the power of a goal.

Make a choice

When adversity strikes, it can seem as though we are out of options. But we always have choices. When the tsunami hits, we can flee or fight. We can react or respond. Whether the adversity you face is economic, physical or spiritual in nature, you have only three choices:

Live with it

Leave it

Change it

If you contemplate these alternatives and decide you are unwilling to live with it (or you've lived with it long enough!), then you're down to either leaving it or changing it. Leaving it might mean surrendering – leaving the job at which you are stuck or failing, walking out of a marriage, or quitting school. If you are unwilling to do that, you have only one alternative left: change it.

Let's assume you are facing an adversity. You have decided that you are going to change it. You are going to fight. You decide to respond positively. You embrace the awareness that if anyone can, I can; if it is to be it is up to me. You set a goal. This is the beginning.

Some people have trouble setting a goal. They can't figure out what they want. They don't really "need" anything. They feel no desire for more than what they have. They can't seem to envision the kind of future they want. Are you one of them? I truly believe that everyone knows deep within what it is that they want, what they desire, or what would make their life better. You may need to work hard to figure it out. In fact, it may require great effort to determine your true goal. It is a worthy investment of time to make because without a goal there is no motivation, and change will remain an impossibility.

Many years ago, Nicki Toombs was a student of mine. She was happily married and had no money problems, as her husband had a good job. I was trying to motivate her to succeed, but she couldn't think of anything she wanted. I asked her dozens of questions and challenged her, saying, "You have a goal in you. We just need to discover it." The more I learned about Nicki, the more I realized how important her faith was to her. She was very active in her church and as I questioned her, she started getting excited about what her success could mean to her congregation's mission of helping others. She imagined donating more money and helping more people. Nicki got specific and wove all the necessary ingredients of a goal together. Her motivation brought her financial success measured by a 700% increase in income. It happened because it was something <u>she</u> wanted.

To determine your goal, you may need to "go to the mountain." Years ago, I learned that getting away from the daily grind and spending some time thinking about what I want and why I want it would lead me to figure out how to get it. Often, I've rented a hotel room for the weekend to do that kind of soul searching. Linda has joked that she knows she's in trouble when we check into a hotel and there's already a flipchart easel in the room! She knows I'm working out our next step and setting new goals.

One of my clients who is successful in the network marketing industry recently sent me an e-mail that said "I'm going to the mountain and not coming down until I have my goals." Are you feeling unsure about what you want? Then get away. Go somewhere by yourself or with your beloved to meditate, to think, to write, to create. Ask yourself, "What would turn me on?" and "What do I want?"

Remember to ensure that the new goal is specific, obtainable, visualized and something you want. When you do, you will get physical energy. Your creative juices will start to flow. You will find focus and direction.

The beginning point of a goal is to analyze your wants and needs. What do you need? What do you wish you had? What would get you excited? This is the starting point. Dream. Ask yourself, "If I had a magic wand and could do anything, what would I choose?"

Another student of mine was struggling. She had set a goal, but didn't feel any motivation. Here she was in a sales career, committed to a sales training program, but failing. Three weeks into the program, she had no production and no energy. I started my questioning process with her and asked, "If you could do anything in life, what would it be?" She said, "I love to travel." So, I made her a deal. I told her if she would produce a specific number of sales within the next 2 months that I would fly her first class to our annual event in Las Vegas. I would arrange for a limo to pick her up at the airport and she would stay at a five star hotel. Her eyes lit up! All of a sudden, she knew what she wanted and what she had to do to get it. She kicked into gear and was energized with enthusiasm. She hit that goal and enjoyed the reward. Then she set a new one.

Motivation comes from an awareness that you want more than you have. When you get specific and set a date for hitting a goal, you will find new enthusiasm and energy. Someone who is dying will live long enough to attend a wedding or greet a new grandchild. Another will endure hardship and fatigue to provide for their family. Goals harness the tremendous power within us to reach for greatness. This is an ancient truth, no less potent today than in 52 A.D. when Saint Paul wrote Philippians chapter 3, verses 13 and 14. He said,

"I give no thought to what lies behind but push on to what is ahead. My entire attention is on the finish line as I run toward the prize."

We push beyond our normal endurance to obtain that which we desire. Goals are powerful. They give us strength and energy. But setting and striving toward a goal is only the first step to self-motivation and changing our lives.

Step Two

Step Two is to <u>make a commitment.</u>

The stronger your commitment, the better the odds that you will stay on the path to your goal. I like to use a breakfast analogy to illustrate this. Have you ever had bacon and eggs in the morning? Next time you do, be sure to look at the plate. The chicken made a contribution. It was the pig that made the real commitment. When you put everything on the line for your goal, you leave yourself no alternative but to hit it.

Yet, this is where so many people give up. This is the point where they discover that the goal they thought they had was only wishful thinking. It's not enough just to set a goal. In order to hit it, you must have absolute commitment. If you are normal, there will be times when the goal you set seems impossible and the steps to reach it seem too difficult to endure. That is when the depth of your commitment kicks in to keep you on track.

Asked to define commitment, I've often said, "Commitment is commitment is commitment." There isn't just one moment that you make a commitment and then you're good to go, permanently. It's almost impossible to commit to forever. You commit. It lasts until you doubt. Then you commit again. It works in marriage. It works in business. It works in dieting. Commit to your goal. Again.

Four ways to deepen your commitment

1. Make a bold statement

You decrease the odds of failing when you announce your goal to others. Whether you hire a plane to carry a banner with your written goal over the sky of your city, wear your wedding band every day, or show everyone a printed 3" x 5" note card upon which your goal is printed, there is great power in telling everyone your goal.

I don't understand why telling everyone gives us the power to hit the goal, but it does. Is it because our pride prevents us from taking the easy way out so we force ourselves to do what we said we would do? Could it be that there is some kind of energy that surrounds us like a force field, drawing us to the people who can provide opportunities, offer direction, or give advice? Somehow, when we tell people our goal, they push us toward achieving it. Even the naysayers' lack of belief in us (or, in some cases their outright ridicule!) can propel our motivation with booster rockets! But only if we allow it to do so. Can you hear yourself muttering, "I'll show you!" under your breath?

For the last 25 years, I've asked my students to set a goal and carry around a large picture of it. I want everyone they meet to ask them, "What's that?" To which they will be forced to reply, "This is my goal". One of my greatest joys is to hear stories from my past graduates about how they hit their goal. Sometimes years pass before I see them again, yet they approach me with shining eyes and tell me about the goal they set during class, then hit. Are you willing to announce your goal to everyone? Will you keep a visual in front of you to provoke conversation and support? If you will, you vastly increase the likelihood that you will succeed.

2. *Have something to lose*

I often tell my students that "fear of loss is a greater motivator than opportunity to gain." Use the fear of loss to prevent you from compromising your efforts toward success. If you don't do the activities that will help you hit your goal, what will you lose? It could be a loss of money. In my programs, I charge a hefty tuition that is subject to loss by anyone who doesn't do their assignments. We use a three-strike system, just like baseball. If you strike out, you cannot attend the remainder of the program nor receive any reimbursement of tuition. For some students, the fear of losing that monetary investment keeps them focused on the goal. For others, it is a fear of embarrassment. When a student is out of the program, everyone on their team, in their office, and their manager knows it. To prevent that, students endure the challenging assignments and continue working toward their goals.

A few years ago, one of my trainers had set a goal and after four months found himself off-track. With love, he was challenged by his peers to determine the worst possible penalty for not hitting the goal. On the same day, he received an invitation to his high school reunion. Since that was a time in his life he had no desire to revisit, he made a vow. He committed to the group that unless he hit the goal, he would attend his class reunion. Not only did he hit the lofty goal, he did it early because he so loathed the possibility that he would have to appear where he had no desire to go.

What would you avoid at any cost? When you have something to lose, you are more likely to do what it takes to hit the goal.

3. Get others involved

Another important way of deepening commitment is to bring other people into it. Bringing your family into your goal enhances your commitment and increases the odds that you will achieve your desired end result. Let's say you have set an income goal based on productivity. You have set a specific date by which you will hit the goal. Telling your son, "Mitchell, when I achieve *this* by *this date*, I'm taking you to Disney World," effectively shuts the door on failure. Mitchell will be bugging you about the trip and you'll have no choice but to do the activities that will allow you to afford it.

I coached a salesperson a number of years who was struggling with hitting her production goal. She was at one of her lowest points financially and energy-wise. I knew we needed to come up with the right goal. The challenge was that she had already set goals. She was working hard and doing "above average" activity. She was a single mother with three children and also a business owner working full time. I knew she had only so many hours in the day! So we began a questioning conversation. I asked, "What would turn you on?" "What would get you excited?" "If everything was paid off, what would you do with your extra money?" Her answer was, "Someday, I'd like to take my children from their home in New Jersey to Hawaii for a vacation." Together, we began to dream. Where would she stay? Would she fly first class or coach? Who else would go on this vacation? What kind of hotel would she choose? She took the answers to these questions and put them into a collage of pictures that she posted in her home. Her best friend and her children knew exactly what she had to accomplish to take them all on this wonderful trip and continuously asked for updates on her progress. That is to say they nagged at her constantly! As a result, they had a wonderful trip that was everything she had envisioned – because she hit her goal!

Before I share the fourth idea for deepening your commitment, I need to warn you that you may not like hearing this piece of advice. It is probably one of the most difficult things you will ever consider applying. In fact, it sort of reminds me of the guy who is walking along the edge of a cliff, and slips. He scrambles to prevent falling into the rushing river 1000 feet below, holding onto a vine. Desperate, he shouts out, "Is anybody up there?" A powerful voice responds, "Do you believe?" Here is a guy who had never prayed a moment in his life, but he shouts back, "I believe! I believe!" The voice thunders a response,

"Let go of the vine." And the guy hollers out, "Is anyone else up there?"

Just because you get a piece of advice, does not mean you want to hear it. Nor does it mean you will actually apply it. But open your mind to the possibility, because here is the fourth piece of advice that will help you deepen your commitment.

4. Remove the option to fail

This is the ultimate way to commit to your goal.

According to legend, when Captain Hernan Cortes landed in Veracruz in 1519, he ordered the burning of his ships before setting out to conquer the Aztec Empire. Such was the depth of his commitment to winning the battle. There would be no retreat. His army was left with only two ways to leave the battle, through death or through victory.

Are there ships in your life that need burning?

That's what I did when I began my full time career as a speaker. Taking a job as National Training Director for a major franchise headquartered in Washington D.C., I made it clear to my superiors and my family that it was temporary. I communicated to them my goal of speaking to an audience of 2300 people by April 16th, 1979. I told them that once I hit it, we would return to Michigan so that I could dedicate myself to becoming a full time professional speaker. When I hit the goal I prepared to leave. In spite of the advance notice, the company offered a tantalizing increase in pay if I would stay. Instead, I moved my family back to Michigan, burned the bridge of security, and began a new career. How could I fail? I couldn't afford to fail. My pride AND my money were on the line. I had to make it work; and I did.

When you keep your options open, it is like having a tug of war while pulling on both ends of the rope. To win, you must let go of one end. A trapeze artist may be reluctant to leap from the security of one swing to the uncertainly of the next, but unless she lets go of the first swing, she'll never make the transition to the second. No one can have it both ways. Have you been trying to hold on to the past while you reach to the future? An absolute commitment to move forward, with no chance of retreat, might be exactly what you need.

Making that commitment helps you figure out how you're going to hit the goal. Initially, the "how to do it" part may not be clear. Make the commitment anyway. Commitment doesn't mean you will "try" to hit the goal. Try to stand up. Right now. Go ahead; try to stand up. You cannot. You either stand up or you don't. There is no such thing as trying. Commit. Then the path will become clear as to how to proceed. As Zig Ziglar has often said,

"If you wait until all the lights are green before you leave home, you'll never get started on your trip to the top."

It is your subconscious mind that will begin guiding your behavior to fulfill your commitment. Set a goal, make a commitment, and then get ready for the third step.

Step Three

Step Three is that you must <u>do the basics</u>. Every goal can be reduced to the basic activities that must be done for the goal to be accomplished. Whatever your position or field, there are fundamental steps taken by those who succeed and not taken by those who don't.

No matter your career and no matter your goal, these are the basics you must incorporate into your life:

Jump in quickly

So much time is lost when we procrastinate at the start of our work. What if instead, you set yourself apart from the norm? What if you formed the habit of starting your work immediately? Skip the little things that take you off-task before you have a chance to begin. Jump right into the work, and do the difficult things first. In most fields, it is the difficult activities that are essential to getting the work done. Perhaps you've heard them referred to as "frogs." If you have to eat a frog, does looking at it all day make it easier to eat? Eat it right away, and the whole day will run smoother and be more productive.

Work smart

Hard work doesn't make you wealthy. If it did, every ditch digger would drive a Rolls Royce because there is no harder job than digging ditches. So what makes us wealthy? It is working smart. That means doing the right things in the right order and completing what you start.

Each day, make a list of the tasks you need to accomplish. Verne Harnish's book, *Mastering The Rockefeller Habits*, describes the effective work habits held by John D. Rockefeller. Running a business that spanned the globe, Mr. Rockefeller began each day with a list of the top five tasks he intended to accomplish. He asked himself, "If I could only complete five tasks today, which five would bring me the best financial return for the time I invest?" From the list of five, he would prioritize which activity to do first, second, third, and so on. Then, he worked at completing the first task. He did not allow himself to skip to an easier item on the list. He worked on the first, most important item until it was finished. If a meeting or phone call interrupted him, as soon as it was done, he went back to that first task.

I've been using this process to guide my daily activity for many years. For the last ten years, I've been teaching it to my students, and call it their *Top 5 Things To Do Today*. I continue to be amazed at its profound results. Often, their challenge is not how to do their job, but how to sort through all the possible ways of spending their time and select the activities that will get them to their goal the quickest. Every morning, they must sit down and select from all the possible activities they could be doing the five most important tasks to accomplish – the ones that will make them the most productive and lead to success in their business. They are required to list them in order of importance and commit to starting with the first task first. What are the most important tasks you must complete? Use the *Top Five Things To Do Today* to guide your work and control your time.

Complete your circles

Simply using a *Top Five Things To Do Today* to determine your activities and placing them in order isn't enough. When I tell the story of John D. Rockefeller, I always implore my audiences to imitate his discipline of placing the tasks in order of importance and to start with the first one. But there is yet another thing he disciplined himself to do. He stayed with each task until it was completed before moving to the next item on the list.

Do you get distracted from completing what you intend to do? Begin at once to change this by changing your thinking. Think of yourself as someone who finishes what you start. From now on, once you start an activity, determine that you will finish it, rather than leave it partially completed. I have often taken a large sheet of paper and drawn half-completed circles all over it. Then I point to the drawing and say, "This is what causes stress." A host of unfinished projects will sap your energy and make you feel defeated. If you try to *complete the circles*, you will find it nearly impossible to put your pen in exactly the right spot so the rest of the circle may be drawn without detecting where the pen was lifted, and it will be slow-going. This illustrates how much faster and more efficient it is to stick with the tasks you start until they are done. Research studies draw the same conclusion. It takes less energy and time to finish what you start than to start, stop, and then re-start. Often, the end result is different once you have interrupted the activity as well.

When you are tempted to come back to a task or project instead of sticking with it until it's finished, remind yourself to complete your circles and be proud of yourself for accomplishing more in less time.

Learn to say "no"

Have you made a list of all the things you need to accomplish in a day? Have you prioritized the list and determined the five most important tasks that would help you to hit your goal? That's a good start, but it takes the ability to say "no" to prevent you from getting off track.

One of the most frequent distractions preventing us from doing the tasks we'd planned is our innate desire to please others. Because we love people, we get off track by saying "yes" to those who wish for us to abandon our priorities in order to do other things.

The only way I know to stop the habit of over-committing and putting our work in second place is to learn to say "no." At first blush, this may seem harsh and cruel. We want to help people, and usually enjoy doing so. It pains us to have to say "no" to someone, and we may feel guilty. Yet, without protecting our time, we can end up becoming a non-profit organization! Do you truly desire to hit your goal? If so, you will need focused attention instead of distraction.

While we want to be of assistance to those we care about, we simply cannot afford to make their goals more important than our own. Like flight attendants remind us each time we fly, "In the unlikely event of an emergency, please place your own oxygen mask on first before assisting others." To do otherwise renders us unable to help ourselves or anyone else. When we are strong, capable and prosperous, we can do the most good for those we love.

If you've put your goal in picture form and posted a thermometer to measure your progress, then you have the necessary ingredients to take control of your time. When someone asks you to do something that will take you off track, I advise you to look at that thermometer and the picture of your goal. If you are on track, say "yes" and do so with joy. If you see that you are behind, simply say these words, "Love to. Can't now." When you are on course or have hit your goal, feel free to dedicate your additional time and energy to other people. When you are off track, stay focused on the goal and allow nothing to deter you.

I'm going somewhere with this...

These three steps – set a goal, make a commitment, and do the basics – are where motivation comes from. Motivation always starts with an awareness that you are not satisfied with the way things are. You think, "I should have more" or "I deserve better than this" or "I'm worth it." That has to happen first. Then you set a goal, which gives you energy. Next, you make a commitment, providing the enthusiasm to reach for the goal you've established and removing the option to fail. Finally, you do the basics consistently. Are you with me so far?

I hope you are committed to making this journey to prosperity and peace. Along the way, I will share the lessons I learned throughout my relationship with Zig Ziglar. Those lessons inspired me to be a better husband, a better father, a better trainer, and a true Christian. Everything he taught me fits into the way that I have come to think and live – what I consider my "process" for a successful life. When he said, "You can react or respond," he was really talking about the awareness we have when adversity strikes. This awareness leads us to setting a goal. Without it, who would set a goal? Because I looked up to Zig and trusted what he said, I took each of his lessons very seriously. Sometimes when I heard them, I realized I had heard that same phrase many times before – but needed to be applying it to my life right at that moment. Often, hearing him re-state the lessons allowed me to reach a deeper level of awareness within myself. I know these same realizations will happen for you as you read.

Some people who successfully change their lives for the better have a "lightning bolt" moment that propels them to making the change. That moment may be quiet – a steady accumulation of discontent until there's a "straw that breaks the camel's back." Other times it is a major personal event, like the death of a parent or child, that causes a re-evaluation of all that has been taken for granted and awakens the desire to change. In 2001, the events of September 11th propelled many Americans to rethink the status quo and change their lives. While these incidents can be painful to live through, major and disruptive change can be the force that leads you to greatness. Whether it is a cataclysmic occasion or the silent dawning of realization, you don't have to face change alone. Take Zig and I along with you. We have prepared the path for you.

Application:

Step One: Set a goal

I have read and reflected on Chapter One. I am choosing to change my life now. I understand that the first step is to set a goal, that is why I have spent time setting a powerful goal for myself. It is a goal, and not a fantasy, because it meets all the criteria of a goal.

My goal is:

It is very specific:

I will obtain this goal by the following date:

This goal is obtainable because:

It is something I want for me. Let me describe how I will feel when I attain it:

Step Two: Commit

A full color picture of this goal is now posted where I see it many times each day. It is in this location:

I know that when other people know about my goal, they will encourage me, so here is a list of those I will tell (and have told):

Here is further proof of my commitment to my goal:

Step Three: Do the basics

I am committed to implementing the basics into my daily life. In addition to those covered in Chapter One, I have added a few customized basics specific to my career and/or situation. On a scale of 1 to 5, here is how I rate myself for each day this week:

(1 is low; 5 is high)

The basics	Day one	Day two	Day three	Day four	Day five	Day six	Day seven
Jump in quickly							
Work smart							
Complete my circles							
Say "no"							

Chapter Three

Keeping Hope Alive

Have you ever felt like you committed to something that was beyond your ability? I remember that feeling of near hopelessness not too long ago.

I should have been feeling confident. As a professional speaker, I've spoken to more than 3000 audiences. I am one of less than 200 recipients of the coveted Council of Peers Award of Excellence (CPAE) awarded by the National Speakers Organization. Yet as I prepared for my first speech at St. Mary's Church for the Men's Group, I was filled with self-doubt.

There was only one thing to do. Call Zig.

He asked me why I felt so fearful. He said, "It's not reasonable. It's not logical." And he told me about the book he wrote to provide hope for those needing encouragement. Have you read it? It is titled, *Embrace The Struggle*.

That conversation got me thinking a lot about encouragement, and I began to reflect on the importance of having encouragers in our lives. I am grateful for the many years that Zig encouraged me. While the words he used may have changed a bit from time to time, his lesson remains the same:

Encouragement is the fuel of hope.

That's what he does best: encourage. During our relationship Zig has inspired me to be a better, more thoughtful encourager. The lesson he gave me that day to help me overcome my nervousness was really an echo of the first lesson he ever gave to me in person. I was so jazzed to be spending that morning with Zig Ziglar, one-on-one, that I felt like my lips weren't even moving! It was over forty years ago, yet I remember exactly what he wrote in the cover of the book he gave me: "Floyd, you're a winner. Keep it up. John 15: 5 – 7." His encouragement stimulated my hope, my belief in myself. I left breakfast with Zig thinking, "I'm a winner." He told me I was, and I believed him!

Keeping hope alive is an ongoing process.

Nine sources of encouragement

Finding encouragement provides the fuel for the journey toward our goals. It forms a strong safety net that will prevent us from despairing during difficult times and helps us to maintain momentum. There are nine things we can do to build the virtue of hope.

1. Improve your self-talk

We can develop a habit of encouraging ourselves by using affirmations. Affirmations are positive statements, said in the present tense that "affirm" or say "yes" to the kind of thinking we wish to take root in our behavior and feelings. The statements may not be true at all, but rather are said as though they are true.

Standing in the grocery store a few weeks ago, I found myself behind a man with a screaming toddler in his shopping cart. The young boy was having a real temper tantrum, with flailing arms and legs, tears streaming down his face, and his shrill voice drawing the attention of everyone in the store. Meanwhile the father was quietly chanting, "Relax, Harold.

Calm down, Harold." Amazed at his composure, I said, "You sure are patient with Harold." He turned to me and replied, "My son's name is Nathan. I am Harold!" Here was a man who used affirmations to control his response to what was beyond his control.

To shape your response to challenges, work at finding a phrase or mantra to repeat so that your mind and your behavior are conditioned to respond the way you desire. For the little-leaguer who is fearful of dropping the pop fly ball during the big game, it may be teaching him or her to chant, "Let the ball come to me! I'm ready to catch it," while watching the batter approach the plate. Standing in the buffet line, someone who is dieting might say, "I choose only foods that are healthy for me." On the drive to a sales call, a salesperson might exclaim, "I am confident, competent, and natural."

Self-talk might also be a pledge or prayer that you repeat often. Archbishop Harry Flynn says, "Come, Holy Spirit, come" whenever he finds himself frustrated or short tempered. Mothers count slowly to ten to remind themselves not to react too quickly to an errant child. Using a repeated phrase helps us choose our response, until the conditioned response becomes natural.

Encouraging yourself with your inner voice is a powerful method of keeping hope alive.

2. Create a visual reminder

Keeping our goals and progress in daily view helps us maintain our belief that we can hit them. Posting a visual reminder is a great tool for self-encouragement.

Dieters can paste a photo of themselves at their desired weight to the refrigerator. Salespeople can use thermometers to track their progress toward a goal. For many years, my students have been required to get a full-color 8.5" x 11" photo of their goal laminated and attached to their key chain so that it would be with them every moment of the day. Personal coaches recommend creating a "dream board" that is a collage of pictures and phrases to inspire action.

When we keep our goals visible and share them with others, we maintain hope from within.

3. *Find encouragers*

Other than my mother, the first adult who really believed in me was Linda's father, Gino Tiracchia. He was a quiet guy; low-key, pleasant and attractive. He didn't say a lot, but when he spoke, he said the right things. I remember one of the most powerful things he ever said to me as though it were yesterday. We were driving through Grosse Point, Michigan, in the land of mansions. Linda and I were in the back seat as we cruised down Lake Shore Drive. He pointed out a big house and in his thick Italian accent he said, "Someday, you're gonna live in a house like that, Floyd". He owned the bar where I worked, and all through those years, and all through my navy stint, I never forgot that proclamation. Because he believed in me, I believed in myself a little bit more. When he died, I asked my mother-in-law if I could have his ring. I wear it often as a visual reminder of Gino's encouragement, and it helps me remember how important it is to be an encourager.

If you had a chance to visit Zig in his office, the first thing you would notice is his Wall of Gratitude. On it, he has placed framed pictures of those he credits with being his encouragers. They are people who believed in him and inspired him to develop the gifts he was given. With an "attitude of gratitude," Zig pays tribute to them with the portraits, remembering their impact on his life. They help him remember the lessons that encouraged him along his life's journey.

Who are your encouragers? Do you think of them with a grateful heart? How did they inspire you to believe in yourself?

4. Use a set of words

Using a set of words can fuel hope in your life. Sometimes the words are given to you, but it is always your choice to make them a part of your thinking or not. Is there a phrase you repeat often that helps you to nourish hope?

An early encourager for me was Dick Aurand. He was the sales manager at Lee Real Estate in Pleasant Ridge Michigan, when I was a young salesman. One day he called the office in Warren. When I answered the phone, he said, "What's wrong?" He didn't even know me, but he detected despair in my voice and made it his business to drive all the way across town to sit down with me and encourage me. Thank goodness he did. I had been teetering on the brink of quitting my real estate career and giving up my dreams. Sacrificing his time and energy to meet with me, he gave me encouraging words that redirected my career. I went back to work with a different attitude and rose to the top of my profession. How did Dick do that in just one meeting? He gave me a set of words to say that would help me to self-encourage. They were:

I am always guided to do and say the things that contribute to my success. Anything that happens - happens in my best interest.

He asked me to repeat that phrase several times a day, until I changed the way I was thinking. I left that meeting and started saying the phrase immediately. I probably said it one hundred times that first day, and another hundred the second day. It changed my thinking and enabled me to turn my career around. It became the basis for the Master Salesperson's Pledge that I've shared with thousands of my students, many of whom recite it daily to self-encourage.

What do you wish to be a "master" of? I assure you, this pledge isn't just for salespeople. It could easily be modified to reinforce any goal from being a "Master Parent," a "Powerful School Teacher," or a "Kind And Loving Spouse." Try it on for size:

I am a Master Salesperson.

As such, I am always guided to do and say the things that contribute to my success.

Each day, I walk and talk like the Master Salesperson I am.

Each day, my Core Values direct my activity.

Each day, I take the steps that lead me closer to my goals.

Each day, when asked the secret of my success, I gladly take the time to share.

From this moment on, anything that happens - happens in my best interest because I am a Master Salesperson!

In the fall of 2010, three of my friends took it upon themselves to find the source of the story they'd often heard. They found Dick Aurand living in Warren, Michigan, and still selling real estate. From the first phone call they knew they'd found a kindred spirit – a man of encouragement and optimism. In fact, during that first conversation, as Ted said, "Have a good day now, Mr. Aurand!" Dick replied, "If you think positive thoughts, positive things will happen!"

That January, they arranged for Dick to surprise me on the platform during our semi-annual event. During the break, nearly everyone in the room came up to meet him and have a photo taken with him. For me, it was a source of delight to be able to thank and encourage someone who had encouraged me all those years ago. The magic of that story is in how many lives he touched by giving me that set of words. It was all because he has the kind of character that doesn't miss an opportunity for encouraging others. One of my trainers said, "Mr. Aurand, we owe you a debt of gratitude. If you hadn't encouraged Floyd that day, none of us would even be here now!"

When we encourage others, it is like tossing a stone into calm water. As the stone hits the water, there is a ripple, then another, and another. Our words and actions can be far-reaching – beyond our ability to even know their effect.

As more than one hundred people came to the stage to have their photograph taken with Dick, I found myself enjoying again and again the joy on his face at being a celebrity at the age of 86. Perhaps he will carry with him the encouragement we gave him that day for the rest of his life. I would like to think so. In the meantime, thousands of my students across the continent begin their day by reciting "The Pledge" to give them encouragement from within, shaping the way they think. Thank you, Dick Aurand!

What set of words can you use to self-encourage? Are there words you could give to someone who needs encouragement from you?

5. Pay it forward

Joe Price spent six years as a pitcher for the Cincinnati Reds. From his youth, people reminded him how difficult it was to get to the majors in baseball. Instead of becoming discouraged, Joe beat the odds and played the game he loves for four major league teams over the course of a decade. Out of baseball now except as a coach for teenage boys, he spent some time running a successful real estate company in northern Kentucky. When he met with one of my trainers, she asked him for advice to give her son, who dreams of becoming a professional catcher. She wrote down, word for word, what he said:

"Don't get too up.
Don't get too down.
You're never as good or as bad as you
think you are."

Her son, Andrew, put those words on a 3" x 5" card and taped it near the light switch on his bedroom wall. When someone discourages him, he remembers Joe Price's story and renews his hope. He often shares that bit of hard-earned wisdom with other players who are feeling manic or off track. Andrew feels proud when he can inspire a pitcher to get back on his game with those few simple words. Did Joe know that his advice would make such an impact in a young man that he never met? When we "pay it forward" we often don't see the influence our words or actions have, but they are there nonetheless, adding another ripple to the pond.

Words are powerful. Our God spoke the earth and its living creatures into existence with His Word. Don't underestimate the power of your words. The future holds many more opportunities for you to inspire and encourage others. Be the one who tosses the stone.

6. *Share your successes*

Were you discouraged from "tooting your own horn" as a child? Most of us were taught from our youth that it's bad manners to brag. By the time we reach adulthood, most of us have developed a tendency to keep our successes to ourselves for fear of appearing arrogant. But sharing them to inspire others is another matter. It isn't "bragging" because we are not trying to communicate that we are better than someone else. In fact, the opposite is true. Are you willing to get past your fear of criticism? Sharing your successes is a gift that helps and inspires if it's done as a form of encouragement.

When something good happens in your life, share it! Sharing good news with our family, friends, and co-workers helps them find the confidence to continue their own struggles. They stop feeling hopeless and are reminded that anything is possible. They may even feel joy.

About eight years ago we instituted the "Good News Award" at my company. Whenever we meet, the team recognizes those individuals who shared their "good news" at least seven times via e-mail over the last quarter. The award itself is the cheapest, funniest-looking award we give. Instead of a fancy plaque or brass statuette (which we award for other accomplishments), it is a little yellow styrofoam ball with a smilee face, mounted on a piece of black marble. Each recipient comes to the front of the room to pose with their award. It is only awarded to those willing to share with the intention of inspiring the rest of the team. We've found that when fellow teammates read the e-mail reports, they are motivated to take action. They think, "I can do that, too!" so they make more calls and get better results. It links our team together and deepens our relationships when we share successes with one another.

Another way of sharing good news is to blog. Have you ever read a blog that is depressing or complaintative? While some may find blogging therapeutic exercises for spouting negativity, I believe it should be inspiring. I write purposefully about things that will encourage others to stretch further, overcome adversities, and seek greater balance in their lives. I try to speak with humility about my own successes and the successes of our team. By encouraging my readers I encourage myself, and lift all of us to a higher plane. Another stone is tossed into the pond!

7. Form or join a group

Trying to succeed alone is difficult. When we surround ourselves with those who encourage us, we accomplish more. I am reminded of the two frogs in the bottom of a pit. One is hard of hearing; the other is not. They are putting supreme effort into jumping out, yet no matter how hard they try, they fail - sliding down the muddy walls to the bottom. Their friends are at the top, shouting. Finally, one of them gives up and dies. The hard of hearing frog can see his fellow-frogs croaking from the rim and their continued presence inspires him to persist. An hour later, he leaps from the pit. When he does, a big brown toad asks, "How did you persist when everyone was shouting that you'd never make it out?" The hard of hearing frog replies, "I thought they were encouraging me!"

Receiving encouragement from others allows us to tap into strength we are often unaware of having. When your workout partner is shouting "three more!" you find strength to do the extra three leg lifts you would have missed had you chosen to work out alone. Our journey to success is often solitary, and the shared inspiration of others who are on the same journey is missed. Yet we are not really alone. When we unite like-minded individuals who have dreams and goals similar to ours, we are able to tap into a higher intelligence for solving problems. The trek toward our goal becomes smoother, takes less time, and feels more peaceful.

Realizing this led me to discover a new method of finding and giving encouragement. My first position as a trainer for a real estate company was lonely. I couldn't really ask my students or my boss to help me figure out how to train more effectively, and I needed objectivity. As a result, I decided to contact trainers at competing firms and invite them to a meeting. We soon realized that we all faced the same challenges, and found that we could take advantage of OPE (Other People's Experience) and one another's knowledge by meeting as a group. For the next couple years, ten of us met regularly to share ideas, problem-solve, and enjoy a bit of camaraderie.

That's the power of a mentor group. You can say anything and you can ask anything. The members agree to confidentiality and trust, and each person makes a commitment to help one another. Does this sound like something that would be an asset to you?

When I became a full-time professional speaker I joined The National Speakers Association. Attending my first annual meeting I forged some new friendships, but soon determined that a convention held once a year didn't carry me through a whole twelve months. I wanted to surround myself with people who would share their secrets, as I was willing to share mine. I founded a group of young speakers who seemed to be "up and comers" and we flew from all over the country to meet quarterly, calling ourselves "The Results Group." We exchanged ideas, brainstormed solutions to problems, and encouraged one another. We were all sitting around talking about all the good stuff during our third meeting when I interrupted the agenda in frustration. "Is it only me that has trouble?" I asked. "Don't any of the rest of you ever have a tough audience or a group that doesn't buy product? You all sound like you don't have the same problems as I do!" That changed everything. It took courage and trust to turn the conversation toward the challenges – but that's where the most learning can happen. Because our meetings became problem-solving sessions, we stayed together for several years.

When we are willing to reveal our weaknesses to one another in a safe environment we can come up with solutions to problems more easily and we can inspire one another. This is the true value of forming a group. You discover you are not alone, and that each person faces the same or similar difficulties. You can brainstorm solutions and learn from each other's experiences. This is the highest and best form of professional encouragement. When you encourage others, you find that they in turn encourage you. Years later, those same individuals went far further professionally than most of our peers. Danielle Kennedy, Mike Ferry and I reached the top of the speaking profession however it's measured – by fees generated, longevity, size of audience, or fame within the industry. What would happen in your life is you were able to join forces with others in a spirit of trust and collaboration?

Mentioning the power of combined effort during his speeches, Zig used the example of the Clydesdales. Strong and mighty, a single horse can pull a wagon many times its weight. When two Clydesdales work together, however, they can pull more than double the load. This is much like the farmer who was trying to get his old blind cow to pull the tractor out of the mud. Stopping by the side of the road to watch, I heard him yelling, "Pull harder, Bessie! Pull harder, Rosie!" Curious, I asked why he was shouting two names, when there was clearly only one cow. He said, "Shhh....Bessie is blind. If she thinks she's doing this all alone, she won't try so hard!"

Compounded effort doesn't just work for beasts of burden. When groups of people pull together to work toward a common cause, incredible things can happen for them!

My business partner and friend, Mike Pallin, discovered a way to utilize the power of combined effort. After experimenting for a couple of years with coaching real estate agents one-on-one, Mike reached the conclusion that most coaching resulted in a predictable outcome. He found that after a while the problems either got solved, leveling out production and diminishing the need for coaching, or the student developed a dependency on their coach, never moving on to self-sufficiency at the level they desired.

Mike's discovery is called R Squared. He takes eight like-minded individuals and puts them on a conference call once a week. Each person makes a six-month commitment to their personal goal and to the group. Each call is highly structured for accountability and learning. The results have been stunning, yet he is simply using an age-old process of uniting people with a common cause to a single purpose. In this case, the purpose is that everyone in the group hit their sales production goal. The students find themselves linked to a group of people they grow to trust and care about. They face adversities; they encourage and support one another. Having a circle of encouragers is far more powerful than having only one! Do you have a group of people who come together to encourage you?

Looking back on all the groups of which I've been a part, I realize that the best gift they gave me was that of encouragement. If you cannot find a group to join, do what I have done so many times in my life: form one.

8. Find a mentor and be a mentor

Another wonderful mechanism for creating encouragement in your life is to find a mentor. Have you considered looking for one? Are you currently mentoring anyone? Often this is the missing ingredient in the attainment of success. All of us need people with whom we can speak truth, share ideas, and brainstorm solutions. Someone on our side. Someone we can count on to "have our back" with no hidden agenda. I like to describe a good relationship between a mentor and a mentee as "the final secret" because it elevates your odds of succeeding in any venture.

Zig Ziglar has been my mentor for over forty years. While the frequency of our conversations has varied, he always encouraged me. When I report how I applied his advice he feels like his investment of time was worthwhile and he is encouraged, in turn, to give me more advice and more of his time.

Mentoring relationships will not endure without encouragement. When the mentee (the one who is being mentored) reports back with the results of having applied the advice they received, the mentor is encouraged to continue giving. There is nothing more discouraging for a mentor than to spend time helping to solve problems and stimulate action only to wonder whatever became of it. Learning how the advice affected the mentee is the stuff that creates deep and long-term relationships.

I usually find myself mentoring between three and five people at once. Terry Sjodin was a mentee of mine some years back. Desiring to be a speaker, she would call me to ask, "What should I do about this?" I'd give her some advice, and she always called me back to tell me what happened. We built such a wonderful relationship that when she suggested we co-author a book about mentoring I was eager to agree. The book became a step-by-step "how to" manual for finding the right mentor, building the relationship, and for being a mentee that the mentor would want to continue to help.

Mentoring has a powerful impact on the lives of both the mentor and the mentee. The Big Brother/Big Sister programs are great examples of the profound impact a mentor can have on a child's life. Self-esteem, school work, and outlook can change completely as a result of building a relationship with an adult who is "ahead in the game" and willing to share their knowledge in a spirit of caring. The reward to the mentor is just as powerful as they "give back" from their stores of knowledge and experience.

What kind of encouragement do you need? We all know someone who is smarter or better at something that we are. Find someone who is "ahead of you" in that area and form a mentor/mentee relationship. It can be a great source of encouragement in your life.

Giving encouragement is a great way to receive it. Most things are like that. Whatever you need more of – offering it to others has a way of rewarding you with exactly what you desire. Do you wish to have more love in your life? Give love. Are you longing for happiness? Make others happy. Do you need encouragement? Give it.

9. *Offer praise*

Have you read The Book of Job? It is a wonderful Old Testament story of a man who was blessed with everything – a wonderful marriage and family, prosperity and position, and good health. Satan tells God that if Job lost it all, he would no longer praise the Lord, but curse him. God allows adversity to strike Job. Losing everything precious to him, Job still praises the Lord. He endures the trials that beset him without forgetting to offer praise and thanksgiving.

However difficult the challenges you are facing, offering praise will encourage you as you encourage others. For some of us, giving praise is as natural as breathing. Most, however, have to choose consciously to become people who praise. We are quick to point out flaws. We notice when something is amiss or someone lets us down, but take for granted the times that things go smoothly. Being someone who praises can be learned. We can teach ourselves to see the good in others, and then to express our gratitude for it. What would happen if you made a conscious attempt to speak positive and encouraging words?

You are an "influential person." Do you speak and behave as though you are? Are you aware that your words and actions shape lives and futures? Because they do. We have all heard someone repeat a comment made to them years before. What statements do you remember that you will never forget? Sometimes those remarks were positive and uplifting, and other times the damage they've done lasted for years. What are people remembering you said that you don't even recall saying?

Each of us can develop a habit of purposefully praising those around us. First, of course, we have to actually *notice* that they or their actions were worthy of praise. Do you have a tendency to focus more on the one thing done wrong than the ten things done correctly? Work at focusing on the ten, instead of the one. Choose to say the things that would lift and inspire others to do better, do more, and see themselves in a different light.

Linda taught me this on Date Night. Every Friday night we carved out time to work on our relationship, often leaving our teenaged sons home for three or four hours. Linda frequently stopped me at the door as we returned and said, "Now, Floyd, don't go in there expecting trouble. If you trust them, they'll go out of their way to prove you right. And if you don't trust them, they'll go out of their way to prove you right." She helped me learn to walk in the door and see the good stuff happening, rather than hunting suspiciously for evidence of wrong-doing.

As parents and grandparents, we can look for ways to express encouragement. The teacher in me wants to jump in and point out the flaws, so that I can help to fix them. But by adding encouraging words, you inspire children to join forces with you. You might say, "You're doing a lot right here. Good. There must be a little hiccup in there somewhere. Let's see if we can find it together." Would the people in your life describe you as someone who is encouraging? Offering to help and solving problems together is a form of encouragement.

Jim Byrnes was a successful Realtor in Palo Alto, California. He was also my friend. I always admired how Jim encouraged others. He had a wonderful gift for saying just the right thing at the right time and for working on the interior. He praised others. During the last few years of his life, Jim really focused on developing his understanding of life and how our choices reflect our reality. Following a coronary bypass procedure during which his heart was beating erratically and he was uncertain about the length of time he had left, he wrote a letter on his ipad to encourage us. Here is an excerpt:

"Remember that failure is not fatal, it is directional. It will transfer you to a much higher level beyond your wildest imagination. I wish I could share all the 'serious' events in my life that I look back and laugh upon. I wish I could share all those people I thought I needed or wanted that were toxic to my growth and wellbeing. I wish I could share with you all the things I wished for and didn't get and now, am so glad I didn't get them.

Have fun with yourself. Laugh with yourself. Learn. Live. And love yourself and others. Let your behavior reflect your commitment!"

Many of the hundreds who gathered at Jim's funeral told stories about how his encouragement impacted their lives. Will you be remembered as an encourager?   By offering encouragement, we encourage ourselves.

Develop the virtue of hope

Hope is not a characteristic that is hardwired into our DNA. It is a virtue to be developed. Of course, no one breaks out in song when they experience adversity. "Yippee! I lost my job!" "Our car needs a new transmission!" "Halleluiah, my bank account is overdrawn!" Do you know anyone who has allowed their adversity to send their attitude into a downward spiral? I am reminded of Charlie Brown's friend, "Pigpen," who didn't like to take a bath. Wherever he went, a cloud of dust surrounded him. While the cloud of negativity may not be visible as such, it is certainly discernable in our posture, facial expression, and voice inflection. But it doesn't have to be that way. We can develop the virtue of hope.

When St. Paul was spreading the Good News throughout the Roman Empire, he wrote to the early Christian communities. Two thousand years later, his letters still provide spiritual nourishment when people need inspiration and hope. They are proclaimed at funerals, weddings and other times people gather for comfort or to celebrate. Countless numbers turn to his messages as they greet or end their day. Among his epistles and letters you will find this message in Romans 5: 3 – 5:

"More than that, we rejoice in our sufferings, knowing that suffering produces endurance, and endurance produces character, and character

produces hope, and hope does not disappoint."

St. Paul is teaching us a powerful truth: our difficulties don't have to stop us. We can use them as a catalyst for hope if we have the right attitude about them.

Facing great hardship, some people continue to bring light to everyone, inspiring all to live with joy and gratitude. When Zig's daughter died of pulmonary fibrosis, he said, "We taught her how to live. She taught us how to die." What a beautiful testimony to a woman who chose not to complain and who chose to remain positive in spirit.

In Houston, a twenty-five-year-old woman attained her goal of getting a real estate license and learning to sell. She was instantly loved for her warmth and for sharing her excitement as she helped her clients buy and sell homes. When she died without warning, everyone in the company was stunned. Though they'd seen her every day, they'd had no idea she was battling terminal cancer. She was positive and radiant, and focused on hitting her goals. She had chosen to live each of her last days with hope and joy.

Can we do that? Live our days the way she did? No matter how much time we have left, these are our last days, are they not? Let's start now. We need to – because our country, our neighbors, our up-coming generations need hope.

When we envision the future as dark, we don't do ourselves any favors. Consider the slew of movies and books that envision the future being filled with violence, poverty and scarcity. Is this what we want our young people to think their adult world will be like? Shouldn't we be thinking of abundance and peace, since what we see and think about becomes reality? Make no mistake about it: Our world needs us. You and I must become beacons of hope.

It doesn't matter what kind of situation we find ourselves in. We cannot wait until everything is perfect in our lives. We need to act now, offering hope and encouragement to those around us. By "paying it forward" we invest in our future and impact how others think and respond. We are the light in the darkness. Offering that light to others allows us to enjoy its brightness as well.

It is impossible to be both hopeful and unhappy.

Develop the virtue of hope.

Be an Encourager. By encouraging others, we encourage ourselves.

Encouragement is the fuel for hope.

Application

Who should be on your Wall of Gratitude?

How did these people encourage you?

Who are the Encouragers in your life right now?

Who are you currently encouraging?

Who should you be encouraging at this time?

What specific action steps could you take to be an Encourager in their lives right now?

Do you need a Mentor in your life?   Who would be a good candidate for mentoring you?

What is your plan for asking this person to mentor you?

Who should you offer to mentor?

The Lessons And The Legacy

Do you realize that within two generations very little is remembered of someone's life? What can you tell me about your great-grandparents? Perhaps you know their names and their origin of birth – but do you know what brought them joy? Do you know the struggles they faced, or their hopes and dreams? Beyond their national heritage, do you know anything about the values and principles they lived by?

The truth is, most of us won't be remembered past our own grandchildren. Of course there are exceptions. Benjamin Franklin, Thomas Edison, Martin Luther King, Jr. But the concept of leaving a *legacy* just doesn't seem to apply to most of us.

This book was written with the intent of advancing the legacy of Zig Ziglar and Floyd Wickman.

Asked to co-author this book in 2008, it didn't take long to realize that neither Floyd nor I are writers. We are speakers, teachers, and motivators; but the crafting of words on a page is a unique and special talent that challenged us greatly. We worked closely every Saturday morning for the first couple years. We manicured each word and audio recorded Floyd's thoughts about his lessons from Zig. After two-and a half years, we had completed the first three chapters. Almost. And Floyd was ready to be done. We decided that I would complete the book at my own pace, so for the next year and a half I listened to the recordings and wrote from my heart.

Floyd and I are a lot alike and have worked together for more than two decades, but we are not the same person, so the final chapters in this book have a different "feel" to them. They really aren't the way "Floyd would say it;" they are more the way "Mary would say it."

I offer these final chapters as a tribute to two men - with a glimpse at how they have lived and thought, and how they desired to be the best that they could be – both professionally and personally. But more, this book is a way to carry their lessons forward into our lives and those whose lives we touch. While our great -grandchildren may discover our blog posts from the early part of this century and feel like they knew us, our true impact on others is in the way we live each day that remains. Remembered or not, the weaving of these lessons into our own lives will leave upon the next generations an indelible mark.

Chapter Four

Joining Forces

Sports teams know that playing on the home field increases their odds of winning. Research proves them right – they do win more often when they play at home. Professional baseball teams win between 53% and 55% of home games. In football, 60% of the games played at the home stadium are won.

It's easy to distinguish the home team. The roar of the crowd feeds energy to the players. Physiologically, that energy creates endorphins so that the players play better, harder and faster. The Minnesota Vikings often call the fans the "tenth man on the field" because the noise in the stadium makes such a powerful impact on the game. They have "home court advantage" - and an opportunity to be their best in front of people that care about them and urge them on.

What does this have to do with you? That the *home court advantage* can be developed in your personal life is one of the most important revelations that I ever had. And whether you choose to do so is completely up to you.

If you have ever heard Zig Ziglar speak or read his books, you would know that he never makes an appearance without mentioning his wife, Jean, "The Redhead." He frequently refers to his family and how proud he is of each of his children. One of his most powerful messages is that to succeed, it is essential to have the "home court advantage." He is passionate about it.

In my desire to emulate my mentor, Zig, I have said something positive about my wife, Linda, during every speech I have given for many years.   His example guided me and has paid big dividends. I always let my audiences know that I am in love with my wife. Those in good relationships identify with me and come to tell me how lucky I am; those in difficult relationships seek advice; those who have heard me before ask after Linda's health – drawing them into a more personal relationship with me. I have tried to demonstrate faithfulness to my marriage from the platform, and to model values and behavior that are counter-cultural in these times. I hope to inspire those who have chosen a permanent partner to fight against the social mores espoused by the tabloids, soap operas and popular television shows that imply faithfulness is the exception, rather than the rule. I want the people in my audiences to strive toward healthy, stable relationships.

My parents surely didn't teach me how to have a happy marriage. My father worked hard and when he came home he wanted to eat dinner and then lay on the couch (the whole couch). My mother suffered from depression. There wasn't a month that went by during my childhood that she didn't threaten to either leave or to kill herself. I don't remember them going out together, or in any way working on their relationship.   In fact, my parents were deeply unhappy most of their lives and their marriage was a reflection of that state of mind. Not exactly fertile ground for a boy to learn how to build a solid, satisfying, life-long relationship.

Do you believe in love at first sight? I got my first glimpse of Linda when I was 21. She was 18. From that very moment, I fell head-over-heels in love with her. She was perfect. Before too long though, the pressures of raising three children, trying to live with the uncertainty of commission income, and my erratic hours were taking their toll. It looked like we were doomed to live apart or in the same kind of joylessness my parents endured.

I was working fourteen hour days, seven days a week, and earning almost nothing. When I arrived home, Linda was exhausted from fending off bill collectors, running the household, and caring for our children. She needed to know where the money was, and I couldn't tell her when the next paycheck was coming in, or even if it was coming in. Our relationship deteriorated. I was committed to her and to our marriage, and I really believed that building a real estate career would pay off. Yet I felt as though I was in a pressure-cooker, both at the office and at home. Can you relate to that?

That's when I invited her to dinner at a little restaurant off 6 Mile Road and Van Dyke. Her mother watched the boys so we could be alone and talk. It wasn't a fancy restaurant but it had great Italian food and was a special place for us. Before we arrived, I rehearsed what I would say. I would tell her I loved her. I would ask her to imagine our future together when the money started to come in. And I would give her an ultimatum. Sitting in that little restaurant, eating gnocchi, I told Linda that I was going to succeed. With her or without her. (I probably chose better words that night.) I asked for her support and explained exactly what I meant. I told her how much I needed her to encourage me and to trust that I was doing everything I could to earn a living. I asked her to come along with me – to the top, and I promised her that if she did she would see the financial benefits. And she agreed.

I look back at that evening as a turning point in our relationship. Everything began to change. Linda's willingness to give me home court advantage made all the difference in the world.

My job titles changed over the years, but the one constant has been having my wife in my corner. I never take her for granted. When I am on the road I call home every night to say good night. If I expect to be traveling for an extended period of time,

I ask for her approval before finalizing my plans. Last summer we were remembering those early days and she said, "All I ever wanted was for him to be happy." The big change was in _me_ – and my ability to communicate the kind of support I needed from her. Once she knew how much her encouragement meant to our future, she became a willing partner. Together, we built a foundation that has grown ever stronger through the years.

Creating The Love Connection

As a professional speaker, I am used to giving people advice about how to build their business and which techniques and strategies will work to accomplish their objectives. Maybe because I am seen as an "expert," I am frequently asked for relationship advice as well. My old friend Art Fettig always said not to be too flattered when someone calls you an expert. An "ex" is a has-been, and a "spurt" is just a drip under pressure! Keeping that in mind, I often joke that Linda and I have our PHD in couples counseling. As the couple. We endured rocky points several times during our 50 year marriage. Yet, in spite of those difficulties, we have a strong and happy marriage. We are frequently complimented for how we demonstrate our love for one another. Let me tell you, there is no way we got this far without learning some lessons. It would bring me great satisfaction to impact your marriage relationship and help you to secure the home court advantage. May I share with you some of the best lessons we've learned?

Set a date

Whenever we are struggling with a problem or situation, we set a date by which we will solve it. We learned the hard way that problems tend to get worse when you allow them to fester for too long, and that most of them don't solve themselves.

Now we know that we need to get help when we cannot figure it out ourselves. Setting a date helps us to have a target. While it is embarrassing to invite a third party into a problematic situation, it would be much more embarrassing to have a failed marriage. Thankfully, I have a spouse who has always been willing to seek help when we need it. Applying what we learned from those counselors has allowed our marriage to thrive.

Have you ever met someone whose relationship is continuously on the brink of disaster? The best way to get through the tough times quicker is to agree in advance that when things get rocky, you will go for help. Set a date. When the target date passes, find a third party to get into the conversation. It could be a counselor, a priest or rabbi, or a therapist.

Hopefully, you are lucky enough to have chosen a partner who is willing to work on problems with you and get advice when you need it.

50/50

Every successful entrepreneur is accustomed to taking control of appointments. We are used to directing activity and solving business problems. Those strategies that work so well in the business world don't translate to your home life, however. In fact, they'll only bring you trouble. Have you seen that in your own relationships? I have learned to remind myself that I have an equal in my spouse, so when things get difficult, it is not just my problem or her problem, but a challenge we need to meet together.

When Linda reminds me, "Honey, it's 50/50," I know what she means. She is reminding me that each of us needs to accept 50% of the responsibility for the cause of the problem. We don't assign most of the problem to the other partner, or resort to blaming. We accept equal responsibility.

Sometimes we wrestle with a problem without even knowing we are doing so. We might express frustration, anger, impatience – or just act crabby! That's when one of us steps forward and says, "I'll take 50%."

When your spouse says those words, there is only one response you can have, "Okay, I'll take the other 50%." Sometimes we take responsibility for what was said, or unsaid; for what was done, or for what could have been done. Never once has either of us been unwilling to accept half of the responsibility.

"I'll take 50%" is the olive branch we extend to one another. It may come after an hour of pouting, but is the beginning of solving anything. It reminds us that we are on the same team and united in the situation. When you are married, you are ONE. There isn't a "you" and a "me" – there is only an "us."

If you were to question every couple that ended up divorced, you'd find that in the majority of cases, one of the two was willing to do anything they had to do to work it out, and the other of the two was putting all the blame on the other. When that happens, the odds of solving a problem become pretty slim. You must realize that if you don't like your situation, you really only have three choices. You can live with it, leave it, or change it. When you are a couple, you decide as a couple whether you can live with it, or if you have to leave it, or if you are going to change it. I truly believe that more people would choose to change it if they understood this.

It's all 50/50.

100/100

The problem is 50/50, but the solution is not. Linda and I agree that the solution is always 100/100. In other words, both of us need to give 100% towards solving the problem. If one of the couple is unwilling to give 100% to work it out, then you are both wasting your time. The only way it works is if it is give and take.

For Linda and me, had we not been willing to give 100% to solving our challenges, I am convinced we would have divorced in 1967. And if not then, the divorce would have happened in 1974 or in 1980. We are indebted to 100/100 because it kept us in our marriage. We always agree that the solution is with both of us. Now, we can laugh while we argue! That's a pretty big difference that this philosophy has made in our lives. But it is not the only one we rely on.

Together we can solve anything

When your relationship is going smoothly, work to keep it that way. One of our most prized possessions is a cheap little statuette of two people hugging one another. It has a special place in our home because it reminds us of a lesson we took years to learn. The caption on the base says, "Together, we can solve anything." Working alone to solve a problem doesn't get the job done. It takes both of you. No one said marriage would be easy. It takes continuous effort to communicate clearly and kindly. It takes work to be patient with one another. Healthy and happy relationships take continuous effort. Begin with an unshakable belief that you are united, that you are in it together. Zig says it this way:

"When a man and woman decide together, you can't go wrong because each has a strength the other does not."

No matter how difficult, the challenges you face together can be resolved - together. This is how permanence is created.

Countables

Of course some of us allow our careers to overpower our personal lives. We work continuously. We bring our work problems home with us. We let our family down by taking phone calls during the time they thought we would be with them. We become preoccupied thinking about work when we are home. Our families may feel as though they are less glamorous or less important if we don't wake up to the fact that we have an obligation to them. If you are a spouse, you have made a promise to love and honor one another until death. If you are a parent, you've committed to teaching and nurturing that child so that they can fulfill their destiny. Those are long-term, far-reaching commitments.   With much trial and frequent error, Linda and I have learned how to do a better job of keeping those commitments. Here is the good news: there are definite actions you can take that will draw you closer together. We call them "countables."

You have probably heard it said that there are only two things you can depend on - death and taxes. Like most "old sayings," this one seems to hold an inherent truth. Life is full of changes. Things we think we can count on turn out to be less solid than we expect.

Families, for example. They are in trouble today. While humans spent thousands of years living within their extended families, never venturing far from home unless their entire family was with them, our society has evolved to a much more transient lifestyle. Siblings may go decades without contact. Divorce rates are somewhere around half of those who enter a marriage. Children are members of blended families and fragmented families. Many are mired in conflict, stress and confusion. So what can any reasonable member of a family actually count on? Only you can answer that.

As you reflect on your answer, perhaps you are admitting for the first time that your family cannot count on anything. That can change. Putting stability into your relationships is the most positive step you can take toward a peaceful existence.

Certainly, the definition of "family" has changed. I saw a wall décor sign that said, "Friends are family that you choose." So, as you read this chapter, please understand that when I speak about your spouse, I am referring to the person most important to you as your life partner. And when I say "children" it may be a grandchild, a nephew or a stepchild. I am referring to the people that you have responsibility for and responsibility to. They are counting on you. Whether they are able to express it or not, they rely on you for constancy.

So how do you put stability into your relationships? I believe it can be done by adding "countables." While I coined that word in my own home, most people can immediately relate to its meaning. What can the people you love can count on?

For most of our married life, we had a single "countable." As a professional speaker, I have flown nearly four million miles. I was on the road and out of town almost every week when my three sons were going to school. I always left home on the last possible flight so we could spend as much time together as possible, and I always returned on the first possible flight to come home. I know speakers who take a couple extra days for a personal vacation in the cities they speak in, but I have always believed that eventually that will get you in trouble or cause your family to believe that they just aren't very important to you. Our first "countable," that I would be home as soon as I could, was my way of showing Linda how important our relationship was to me.

Date night

Do you remember the anticipation you felt back in high school when you had a date with your sweetheart? You looked forward to being together and spending time alone. It was Date Night.

Once married, the decades fly by, and we tend to grow a bit careless with one another. Children take the focus off the marriage relationship, and husbands and wives may begin to take one another for granted. We stop *courting*. While that word is used infrequently today, it is an apt description of a relationship we desire to deepen. It describes a relationship that is full of hope. Courting is when we put our best foot forward, trying to impress upon our love to choose us forever. And my big brother Zig advised,

"Never stop courting each other."

Friday night is Date Night at the Wickman house. To demonstrate our commitment to one another, Linda and I have carved out an island of time when we put one another ahead of everyone and everything. We set aside time to be together and work on our relationship every single week. This has made a huge difference in our closeness. Because it's been so important, we rarely allow anything to be scheduled over it.

I don't mean to say we go out on the town every week. When our kids were small, we went out for dinner sometimes. As someone who has spent most of my life traveling, I relish the time I have at home with my wife. So, as empty nesters, we often spend Friday evening there. We usually start with some wine, choosing a pair of wine glasses from our collection that best describe the mood we are in. Sometimes we begin with a little argument. That gives us a chance to say what has been on our minds or to talk about something that has been bothering one of us. Then we begin "our time." We count on it.

When we lived on Lake St. Clair and had a boat at the end of our dock, we frequently had friends that stopped in unannounced. I always enjoyed that, except on Friday nights. To protect our time, we put a flagpole at the end of the dock. If the green flag was out, "come on in"; if it was yellow, "please call first"; and if it was red – "don't bother stopping, it's probably Date Night!"

What message are you sending your mate when Date Night is in your weekly rhythm? You are proclaiming with your words and your actions that there is nothing more important than one another. You are providing a "countable" in a world of UNcountables.

For the family

Families need countables, too. Some years ago, I coached a young man who had built a successful real estate practice with his wife. Between April and July of 2007, the market shifted and they found themselves grappling with 20 properties that were scheduled to close but did not – at a loss of five million dollars in production. In addition, Jim's dad moved into their home as he battled cancer. It was a tough time to think about creating balance, and Amy often felt she was on her own dealing with their family life. Their young daughter, Emily, was engaged in softball several times a week, and Grandpa needed his family's daily assistance.

Jim deeply loved his family, yet they felt as though they were always in "second place" as he took phone calls from the clients he had promised, "I will always be available to you." He was working long hours trying to strengthen his financial position so he didn't want to neglect a call. Answering the phone meant he would leave the dinner table or miss most of the softball game, sending the message to his family that "work" was more important than spending time with them. That's when I taught him about "countables."

The Galligans started small. Every Sunday morning, the family would attend church together and then go out for breakfast. All of Jim's appointments were scheduled for after twelve noon. Sunday mornings became a time that his family knew they could count on Jim's presence, no matter what else was happening. From there, they expanded structured family time to one evening a week to be together. Jim left his phone on, but began screening his calls, so that he only responded to offers on his listings and to emergencies in his business.

He learned that when he put his family into his schedule, he could look forward to a time to just be a human being rather than a "real estate robot" (his words). That small start gained momentum and he credits his better-balanced life with his soaring success. Jim looks forward to his family time because it is scheduled in. Those LFT's (things to "Look Forward To") give him energy and motivate him to keep working so he can enjoy his time off without guilt. Today, he attends every game, arriving on time with his wife and daughter – having scheduled her games two and three months in advance. Everything is planned into his weekly calendar, and he doesn't let anything get in the way of his pre-arranged family time. Jim and Amy schedule date night twice a month, and his voice message says,

"If you are calling after 6:00pm, I will be returning calls promptly at 9am tomorrow morning." That gives him the option of calling back sooner, yet doesn't over-commit to the caller. The Galligans have just had their most productive real estate year on record, and while they consider balancing work and business an ongoing journey, they are grateful for the peace that "countables" has brought to their lives.

As you can see, it is not only the individual that benefits from "countables." When we schedule important people and routine events into our lives, the whole family can "settle in." They know that they have 100% of our attention and that nothing is going to change that. They begin to see that family time isn't just measured by quantity, and they learn to enjoy the quality of being given undivided attention. What are the "countables" you need to add to your schedule?

Romance

How long ago did you fall in love? Were you a romantic suitor? Whether you got lessons from a friend or found it all just came naturally, as time goes by, it is easy to fall into a comfortable relationship and to postpone the little things that can keep romance alive.

Adding romance is like adding that special spice to spaghetti sauce that gives it zing and sets it apart from anything else. Rather than just being roommates for a few decades, what if you lived with your lover? Look for opportunities to rekindle the love affair in your marriage. What kind of things could you do together that would add romance? Sharing a glass of wine or a bubble bath reminds you both of the attraction you have with one another. Can you recall the last time you had a candlelight dinner at home? Whose idea was it?

Linda and I hold hands often. We sit beside one another to watch a movie, snuggled under one of Linda's quilts. We speak kindly and say "please" and "thank you." Romance isn't one big event with rose petals strewn across the bed. The target is not to create a more satisfying sexual relationship – though it may do that. The goal is to deepen the love connection, and add flavor, dimension, stability and peace to your world.

Say "I love you"

Did you hear about the man who loved his wife so much that he almost told her? While that might be a funny line, it would be unfortunate if there were too much truth to it, don't you agree? We often repeat the behaviors of our upbringing, so for those of us that didn't hear "I love you" said to us or to others, love can be hard to express. What a shame it would be if we saved those precious words for only special occasions. Too many people don't say them at all.

There's an old story about a long-married couple riding together down the road. The wife says to her husband, "Remember when we were first married and we used to sit all snuggled together in the front seat when we drove?" The husband looks over at her and replies, "Well, I ain't moved!"

Then the wife says, "But, Honey, do you still love me?" He answers, "Of course I do. I married you, didn't I?"

How often do you say, "I love you"? Are those you love expected to know that you love them without actually hearing you say the words?

Let your love be apparent to everyone through your words and actions. On the way home from a visit by one of my trainers, her young daughter said, "Floyd and Linda really love each other, Mommy." Is your love evident in your daily behavior? I would suggest that you develop the habit of saying "I love you" often. At breakfast one morning in Dallas, Zig told me that the first words out of his mouth every morning when he speaks to Jean is "I love you." Recently, he's begun saying it to me when I call him. What an incredible feeling to hear Zig Ziglar say those words.

Our strengths are our weaknesses. I remind the people that work for me that they never have to wonder what is on my mind. Sometimes that makes them cringe! I just have to tell them when I am disappointed or angry. That weakness is also a strength because I just have to tell them when I am pleased or pleasantly surprised, too. This characteristic has seeped into all my family relationships as well. What value is there for them not to know that I love them?

I have learned to say "I love you" a lot. It is a grand thing to express love, but I also compliment skills and commitment. As I do it more, I hear them make more loving statements to one another.

Over the last couple years, this habit has spilled over into my business life. I've found it easier to tell my partners and my trainers that I love them. I always have; I just didn't think it was appropriate in a business relationship to say so. Shouldn't all the people you love have the opportunity to hear you tell them so? The phrase "I love you" has a way of becoming contagious. At the end of our company conference calls, the president asks for positive parting words. This allows each participant to express gratitude for something or someone or offers words of encouragement if they so desire. You wouldn't believe how often the final moment of the call is ten or twelve people all saying, "Bye! Love you guys!" It's probably not a coincidence that most of the members of my team have been together a long time. I believe that reminding them regularly that they are loved and appreciated has been a major reason that their loyalty to me, to one another and to the company runs deep.

Tell her she is beautiful

Have you ever chatted with an elderly man who indicates his wife and says, "Isn't she the most beautiful woman in the world?" Len and Ro Jambor had that kind of relationship. Whenever Ro left the room, Len would lean forward and praise her beauty, her heart, or her grace. He was madly in love with her until the day he died at age 91.

What is beauty? My wife is beautiful. Her eyes sparkle. I know every nuance of her smile. I love the way she tilts her head when she listens thoughtfully. She is always so concerned for other people. She is frequently intuitive. These are the characteristics that make her a beauty. I often tell her, "You are getting more beautiful every day."

By speaking those thoughts aloud I have added another dimension to our romance. She knows I see her inner and her outer beauty. How does that affect her attitude? What role does that play in her effort to keep herself trim and healthy? Does it make her feel more secure in our relationship? I believe the answer is a resounding "yes." Saying these words is not a technique or strategy. I honestly feel this way. If you need to rekindle romance – work on your attitude first, and then try saying what you are thinking!

Post It notes

Do you have little yellow stickee notes in your desk? Have you ever thought about them as a tool for building your relationships?

Linda and I drink coffee in the morning. I am up first and working at my desk by the time Linda gets into the kitchen. We frequently leave one another a little note, using a yellow Post-It and sticking it to the cupboard, the coffee pot, or a favorite cup. Sometimes it's as simple as "Love you, Honey!" but the one that says, "Sorry I was so grumpy last night. Have a happy day!" is the one Linda saves. She has collected them on the inside of the kitchen cupboard near the window, so I know which messages have spoken to her heart. They reiterate our love for one another, and bespeak of thoughtfulness. In only a moment we have put a smile on our beloved's face. What a wonderful way to start the day!

Like and respect

It's one thing to be in love, but it's quite another to "like" our partners. A fourth grade boy came home from school to share with his father what he had learned about marriage. He says, "Did you know that in some parts of Africa, a man doesn't know his wife until he marries her?" The father replies, "Son, it works the same way here in America."

Have you spent time learning to really know and like your spouse? I mean really "like," as opposed to "love." Love is a wonderful emotion, but marriages need more than love to keep them healthy. The world is full of divorced couples that loved one another, but couldn't maintain a marriage. Love cannot solve everything. You must also like and respect one another. We've all heard the saying that "opposites attract." Over time, those opposite characteristics so admired in the early years can become a source of dislike and frustration. Accepting your differences, rejoicing in them, celebrating them – that Is the secret.

Respecting one another means honoring the uniquenesses, those personality quirks that differentiate us. The Chinese have two special words that describe this opposite orientation. They call it ying and yang. It is the two halves that make up the whole and complete one another. It is found everywhere in the natural world. Interpersonal relationships would be boring and stifling if not for our differences. It is those differences that allow us to complete one another. When we respect our partner and stop trying to change them, we honor those things that make us different. And our perspective begins to shift.

Six strategies that deepen the love connection

What can you do that will put the "like" back into your relationship? Here are six strategies we use to deepen our bond to one another and contribute to the home court advantage.

1. Worship together

I was well into adulthood when I began to attend church on a regular basis. My best friend, Mike Yurek, invited me to go to church with him and I went for only one reason: so that I could join him for breakfast afterward. Week after week I listened to the sermon accidently, and only because it came before we could head to the restaurant. That clergyman had one recurring theme that got me hooked, though. It was the concept of peace. For all my successes, I had always felt a stirring of dissatisfaction and unease. Can you relate to that? I realized that what I was missing was peace, and I set after it with the enthusiasm of a parched man pursuing water. From there, I began to enjoy my success more. I could see the hand of God in my past and in my future. I started to read the Bible. And I wanted to share this newfound peace with my dear wife.

Linda had stopped going to church decades earlier as our boys were confirmed. She wasn't interested in going to breakfast with my guy friends on Sunday mornings, but I had a great desire to experience worship with her at my side. Because she likes and respects me, we began attending mass at St. Mary's near our home. We sat in the same pew each week, and gradually got to know those around us. We began to get involved. Linda joined a quilting club. I bought a bicycle so I could ride with the Men's Group on Saturday mornings. And I started taking notes during the sermons – just like my brother, Zig. I started reaching for that peace they talked about so much from the lectern.

There is a special closeness that Linda and I have experienced as we hold hands from the parking lot to the church door. We wave greetings to new friends. We feel like we've found a place there. And we have something more in common – a shared experience of the song, the prayer, and the relationships that we wouldn't have if we hadn't begun to worship together.

Just prior to attending church together, I had sold my business and was flush with cash. Yet looking back, I clearly recall this as the time we were the unhappiest in our relationship. Everything changed when we began going to church each week. I finally realized that while I had been out searching desperately for peace, it had been right inside of me all the while. When we focused on that message, and began feeding it so that it would flourish, our home and our marriage became peaceful.

This is not a uniquely Wickman experience. An article in the prestigious American Sociological Review said that attending worship together makes you happier. Chaeyoon Lim, assistant professor of sociology at the University of Wisconsin-Madison, led the study that "offers compelling evidence that the social aspects of religion...leads to life satisfaction."

Could shared worship bring you closer together as a family?

2. *Express appreciation*

When Linda is frying her famous corn fritters, I stop in the kitchen to let her know they smell good and that I am looking forward to eating them. I tell her, and anyone who will listen, that she makes the best corn fritters in the world. In the business world, we teach managers to praise in public and criticize in private. That's pretty good marital advice, too! Look for opportunities to pay sincere compliments to one another, and say them loud enough for others to hear.

Saying thank you for routine tasks, and for the effort put into doing the household chores, can be difficult to remember. We have a tendency to take them for granted. Say thank you - even if the end result isn't the same as if you'd done the task yourself. One of my students shared how much her spouse was trying to help around the house while she was focused on building her business in my class. Her husband sorted laundry, and then began to fill the washer when he ran into a problem. He shouted, "Honey, what temperature should I use to wash my sweatshirt?" She hollered back, "What does it say on the shirt?" His reply: "University of Michigan!"

Instead of frustration or anger, what if we felt gratitude for a helpmate that attempts to help? What if we could laugh with one another in gratitude for our differences? Certainly, we would live happier lives. Express your appreciation.

3. Listen with your eyes

Are you a good listener? German philosopher Paul Tilley said, "The first work of love is to listen." Listening is not the same as "hearing." You may hear the message, but if your attention is elsewhere or your response is frequently a tepid, "Mmmm," you are not listening with your eyes. Making eye contact with the speaker is respectful. The next time someone begins telling you a story, turn all of your attention to him or her. Look at their eyes, watch the expressions in their face, smile and nod encouragement as they talk. Paying 100% attention to the person speaking is a way of honoring them. It makes them feel important. And they are important! Stop what you are doing, make eye contact and really listen. If that is not possible, ask them to wait until you can give them your full attention. This is one of those things that takes some practice before it becomes a natural habit. That is especially true if you have a habit of multi-tasking or have married someone who runs a continuous monologue. You may need to remind yourself to listen carefully, even if you are uninterested in what is being said. Why? Because listening demonstrates love.

4. Give it a number

"Are you hungry?"

"I don't know. Are you?"

"I'm kind of hungry."

"When do you want to eat?"

"I don't know. Not yet."

Or

"Do you want to see a movie?"

"Do you?"

"Kind of."

This kind of blasé dialogue takes its toll on me. I want to know what you think, or I wouldn't have asked! Linda and I solved this one, too. In fact, it delights us to hear others copying our solution.

I've always said that numbers take all the guesswork out of the equation, so we created a scale of one to ten we use to communicate opinions. Instead of asking, "Are you hungry?" we ask, "On a scale of one to ten, how hungry are you?"

"I'm a five."

"Okay, I'm an eight. When you are an eight, let me know and we'll eat. Fair enough?"

This is especially fun when we entertain our grandchildren. They love taking a survey of everyone in the room and reporting the numbers so we know when to start grilling the burgers! At the same time, every voice is heard and respected, so no one feels left out or railroaded into doing something that isn't in everyone's best interests.

5. Get out of the trap

Do you argue about the same things over and over? Are you frustrated with that and ready to make a change? Repeating the same patterns of negative behavior takes us down the same path of conflict we've been on before. I would urge you to take a look at the communication traps you consistently fall into. What do you argue about? What are the triggers for that argument? Which of the two of you seems to care most passionately about that particular issue? Once you know that, you are on the road to solving the problem.

Having moved 28 times in 48 years, we always employ a decorator to help us make a new property into our home. The decorator works with Linda, then I come onto the scene to give my opinion. Unfortunately, this became a source of great conflict in our marriage. To solve the problem, we learned to divide our decisions. While I want and need to express my opinion, ultimately it is Linda who cares the most about the outcome and is responsible for implementing the decorating plan. We agreed that I would look at the samples and colors after the initial selections were made, then Linda says these four words, "I'll consider your input." That phrase helps us to avoid arguing about who is right and reminds me that we've agreed it is Linda's decision that will be acted upon. I feel good because I gave my opinion and it was listened to; she feels good because she is not making choices all by herself. Best of all, we avoid the same old meaningless conflict.

Take some time to examine the most frequent triggers for conflict in your relationships. Who has the strongest feelings about the subject? Decide who should be responsible for the outcome. Then create a communication mechanism to remind one another what was agreed upon. A phrase like "I'll consider your input" is neutral and respectful.

Consider the bridegroom who asks his father's advice. He says, "You and Mom have had a great marriage. What's the secret?" Dad's reply is, "Early on, we decided that I would make all the big decisions, and she would make all the small ones. It's worked out great for us. Of course, so far, there haven't been any big decisions...."

Communication mechanisms go a long way toward creating peace in your relationships. Using either a phrase or a numbering system will help you avoid the most frequent triggers for frustration and conflict.

6. Watch for their passion

When the people we love develop a passion for activities and interests that we don't share – the barriers can go up, preventing the love from flowing freely and creating conflict. As a late teen, my oldest son, Floyd, was motorcycle-crazy. The thought of him on a bike gave me nightmares and I was filled with fear for him. I envisioned an accident that would cripple or kill him. This is probably a familiar lament for many parents. While our goal is to raise independent children that make good decisions and live in happiness, it can be difficult when their choices seem destructive or nonsensical. Once Floyd bought his first motorcycle, though, I knew the time for talking and worrying was over. I had to find a way to live with it.

Linda and I went out and bought him a helmet, which we gift-wrapped in a big box and decorated with a bow. Can you imagine his face when he opened that gift? He knew in an instant that we respected him and had accepted his choice in spite of our reservations. We cared more about him than about our fears. It was Dr. Wagonheim, our marriage counselor, that taught us a phrase we live by:

"Caring about what others care about is what caring about is all about."

I learned a valuable lesson because I was able to set aside my own concerns to put Floyd Junior and his feelings first. My son escaped unscathed from his biking years, fortunately, but we showed true caring by standing with him even though we didn't agree.

The same effort needs to be put into marriage, as well. Do you make it a practice to actively look for ways to demonstrate caring?

Linda is a quilter. She has an artistic sense of color and texture and loves creating handmade quilts to give to special people in her life. At last count, she's made over thirty unique quilts. For Christmas one year, I imagined photographing them to make a keepsake for her. I began by contacting the people to whom she'd given a quilt and asking to borrow it. I invited them to write a letter to Linda about what the quilt means to them and how they use it. Months in advance, I enlisted the help of Linda's best friend, Rosie, to arrange for a "Girls Day Out" so that I could have the quilts professionally photographed. My son, David, is a graphic artist. He laid out a coffee table book featuring each quilt in full color, placing the personal letter on the opposite page. Throughout Christmas Day, Linda had several bouts of happy tears for the unforgettable gift she received. That book showed her the depth of my caring by demonstrating how much I cared for her quilted creations. Investing time and thought into surprises and gifts can bind a husband and wife together and demonstrate their love for one another. Remembering these actions soothes relationships during difficult times.

Keep your eyes open for your partner's passion. Let them know you support their activities. This is the ultimate way of strengthening the foundation of your relationship. It authenticates your respect for their choices and your joy that they are doing something that they love to do.

During these last few years, Zig and I have spent hours on the telephone sharing stories, ideas and thoughts. Though the phrase has always been used in sports, he coined the term **home court advantage** as it applies to one's personal life. And while he has spoken about the importance of this topic frequently, I have known for decades the value of courting my spouse and demonstrating my love for her. My incredible marriage has given me a deep understanding of the immense power of love and of the impact a peaceful home life has on every facet of an individual's circumstances. In First Corinthians, Chapter 13 we are reminded:

"Love is patient, love is kind. It bears all things, believes all things, hopes all things, endures all things. Love never fails."

Isn't this what we all long for? What would it take for you to build a stronger home court advantage? If you examine the way you have been loving, does it exemplify what St. Paul describes, or do you have a ways to go? Are you willing to nurture and develop your relationships so they epitomize the love in Paul's epistle? Are you expressing your feelings aloud? I recommend that you arrange for a conversation about this chapter with those you profess to love. Share suggestions you think could improve your relationship. Open your heart, suggest a change in behavior, and commit to one another. This will be a difficult assignment for those with a life-long habit of not speaking about emotions and feelings, but it isn't impossible. I recall one advisor who counseled me with this lesson: "Floyd, she cannot read your mind!" You can't expect your partner to read your mind – though sometimes it seems like s/he should be able to do so! You must talk to one another, listen to one another, and keep the romance alive. If you haven't been doing this already, you can start any time. It's never too late.

How much longer do you wish to leave your relationships as they are? What will your future hold if you choose to ignore this message? I urge you to take action now. Use these tools to develop and deepen your love connection. The home court advantage gives you the foundation upon which to build a future worth looking forward to.

Application

Are you willing to work toward building your home court advantage?

Using this chapter as a guide, how would you rate your current home court advantage on a scale of 1 to 10?

Schedule a meeting with your spouse/significant other to get agreement on the 50/50 and 100/100 Rule. Agree that you will remind one another about this when necessary.

Commit to doing at least three action steps that will nurture home court advantage.

_____ Say "I love you" often

_____ Leave Post It notes

_____ Worship together

_____ Express appreciation

_____ Listen with your eyes

_____ Give it a number

_____ Get out of the trap

Common traps in your relationships:

What are some ways you might be able to "get out of the trap"?

What are your spouse's/children's passions?

How can you support those passions?

What characteristics make your spouse beautiful/handsome?

Put a note in your planner to revisit this page in two weeks to check your progress and commitment. Put another reminder note in your planner for 45 days out to do the same.

Chapter Five

Self-Talk

Words have power. They can stir hearts, inspire nations, and win victories. Even words that have never been written nor spoken aloud have power. These unspoken, yet powerful words are called "thoughts." And one of the greatest revelations you can have is to understand that you can choose what kind of thoughts you have.

Imagine! You can choose to build yourself up or to tear yourself down. You can choose whether to persevere in the face of adversity or to abandon the dream. It's your choice! Often, that choice is made without a sound. You may not even be conscious of making it. That's because far more important than the words that others speak to you are the words you speak within your own mind. Start paying attention to what you are saying to yourself. What do you hear?

My first awareness of this incredible concept came early in my sales career when Dick Aurand gave me the powerful affirmation that I shared with you in Chapter Three. That affirmation turned my whole career around because I convinced myself it was true. Of course, at first, I was just saying the words without believing their truth. But with frequent repetition - my thinking changed. I started to stand a little straighter. I began feeling more optimistic. I started trusting that I would do and say things that would contribute to my success. I experienced a personal transformation that gave me the unshakable belief that not only *can* I control my thoughts, but that I *must* control them in order to succeed. I want you to have that same transformation in your life!

For over three decades, I have been at the helm of a training company that gets the best sales results in the history of the real estate business. While the techniques and strategies are powerful, if we didn't work on the students' thinking, our results would be considerably less. Since 1979, every class has contained a component of positive affirmations to help control the students' subconscious thoughts. It may be singing a song, or saying an affirmation, like, "If anyone can, I can!" I've had many groups recite a pledge. Verbal affirmative statements, said repeatedly, direct future thoughts and perceptions. Could you use that in your own life right now?

Consciously speaking affirmations enables us to shape the way we think. But what about all the times we speak without conscious thought? What about all the statements we make without forming the message purposefully? UN-consciously saying affirmations has just as profound of an affect on our thinking. Perhaps even more so.

When Zig and Jean and I had dinner in Dallas, Zig asked me how many books I had written. When I answered "seven," I felt pretty pleased with myself. After all, for a kid that didn't make it through ninth grade, that's not too bad! Most of my books had been written for salespeople and for sales managers in the real estate industry, (though I had written one novel, *Letters to Linda*). I also counted my first book, though it never sold very many copies and was out of print. (Probably because of the title: *Dead At 30. Buried at 72.*) So, while seven isn't very many compared to all the books Zig has written, at least I had an answer to give him beyond one or two.

That's when Zig said, "You need to write more books. It's a sure way to leave your legacy."

"I'm working on a book now," I assured him, "but at the rate I'm going, it's going to take forever!"

And his reply?

"Keep saying that, and it will."

Now, of course I KNEW THAT! In fact, my very first thought was, "I know!" But there I was, going against everything I know about positive affirmations and affirming the negative instead.

That conversation really got me thinking. For a long time, I have wanted to write a book about all Zig Ziglar has taught me. Being blessed with this incredible relationship with him created the desire to share how I have applied his lessons. Yet I had not written down more than a couple of bullet points on a legal pad. I decided to set a date and find a writing partner that would help me stay on track. Of course, I also committed to control the way I was talking to myself about writing that book.

On the platform, I am known as a self-help guru. Nominated twice as "Entrepreneur of the Year" in Michigan (I came in second place) and chosen one of the "Top 25 Most Influential" people in the real estate industry, I have built a pretty successful career around teaching Realtors to succeed. While they learn many powerful techniques and dialogues, I always begin with a lesson on thinking. I try to convince them that "If anyone can, I can," and that they need to act and think like a top producer in order to become one. If a person doesn't start working on the interior first, the exterior - their environment and their results - isn't going to change for them.

For over four decades I have read every self-help book I could get my hands on. As a result, I like to visit local bookstores whenever I travel. Do you?

Approaching the help desk recently, I inquired, "Where is your self-help section located, please?"

The clerk replied, "If I told you, it would sort of defeat the purpose, don't you think?"

Go to the largest bookstore in the world – Amazon.com – and enter "being successful" into the search box. Check out the selection there and you will find the common denominator in all of them is that successful people think positively and speak positively.

You will also find one of my early favorites, *As A Man Thinketh*. Have you read it? This old, thin volume speaks very simply about the power of thought. It changed my awareness of those thoughts and words rambling around in my head. The title expresses the concept: "As a man thinketh in his heart so is he." Our thoughts mold our environment, our character, and our destiny. Our thoughts can be chosen to shape the kind of life we wish to have. This simple principle changed the life of my best friend.

Mike Yurek

As a young sales manager, I hired and trained a salesman who, over the years, became my best friend. When I started Floyd Wickman Associates, I asked Mike to head up my product sales division and he did a pretty good job. One evening, he revealed his feelings of disappointment in himself. The way he saw it, I was successful and prosperous, and while he had worked just as hard, he was stuck earning so much less. He reminded me that he was the one that won the "Best Presentation Award" in the Dale Carnegie class we had taken together, and that I had come in second place. He recalled that he was the one who broke our company's sales record. He looked at his past and asked in frustration, "How come Floyd is doing so well, and I am not?"

After listening to this litany for a while, I finally spoke. I said, rather forcibly, "Mike, the only difference between you and me is that I see myself being successful and having the things I have. You wish it. But you don't see it. Everybody wishes they had more, but to get it, you have to see yourself having it." Later in the week, I gave him a copy of the book, *As A Man Thinketh*.

The following year he earned his first-ever six figure income. That conversation got him committed to work on his thinking, and enabled him to turn everything in his life around. As Joel Weldon says,

"Success comes in cans. Not cannots."

Changing the way we think, changes the outcome of our lives.

Success comes in cans

How many people do you know that built a life for themselves by thinking successful thoughts and believing they could have what they want? They may have even reminded other people to think positively. Suddenly, though, these are the same folks who find themselves seasoned citizens who have lost the security of employment or watched their retirement savings vaporize before their eyes. I hope at least one of them is reading this book right now.

If I am talking to you, then you need to be reminded of your own inner power. You already possess everything you need to succeed again. Do you believe that?

How you think has everything to do with the circumstances in which you find yourself. If you wish to change your destiny, change the way you are thinking. It brings me great joy to tell you that it's never too late to change the way you think! Your thoughts determine the words you use when you talk to yourself. So, what has your inner voice been saying to you lately? You have been listening, whether you realize it or not. What do you hear?

Lisa and Antoinette are students who have attended dozens of my speeches and events. A few years ago they gave me a plaque, saying, "This reminds us of what you always say." On the plaque is engraved these words:

"Watch your thoughts, for they become words.

Watch your words, for they become actions.

Watch your actions because they become habits.

Watch your habits because they become character.

Watch your character because it becomes your destiny."

I memorized that statement and have used it many times on the platform to express my belief about the power of thought. I believe to my very core that our thoughts become our destiny. Every one of us is living proof of that.

That same message is in the oldest self-help book of all: The Bible. (B-i-b-l-e is actually an acronym for Basic Instructions

Before Leaving Earth). I love the Book of Proverbs. Its ancient wisdom is just as profound today as when it was written thousands of years ago. In Proverbs chapter 17, verse 7, we read:

"The mouth of the fool works its owner's ruin; the lips of a fool are the snare for their owner's life."

The words we speak have power. They can bring us success or they can defeat us. Negative thoughts catch us in a snare that binds us in hopelessness and failure. Destructive thoughts become words that we speak to ourselves and then to others. They lead to our ruin. We must continuously strive to eliminate negative self-talk. We must be vigilant in controlling what we think and say.

That's easier said than done. The habit of saying something negative is insidious. Have you ever tried to recall someone's name? When we are having difficulty pulling something from our memory it is common to say, "What is his name? I can't think of it! I'm just not coming up with it!"

What a self-stopping thing to say! How can we possibly ask our memory to come up with the name, when we've just told ourselves not to? And that's just a simple example. There are so many times we say negative things to ourselves without even realizing we are doing it. Why is that important?

Maxwell Maltz, author of the book, *Psycho-Cybernetics,* taught us that the brain is a goal striving mechanism. It doesn't have emotion. Your brain doesn't say, "That's a negative statement, and it's really not true" or "Oh, yes you can!" It accepts as truth whatever we bring to it. Give it a goal, and the brain (the mind) goes after it as though it is true. So, when we say, "I can't think of it", we are instructing the mind not to think of it. We are giving it a negative goal.

All day, every day, you are engaged in a silent conversation in your mind. That little voice is chattering away inside and you are hearing it, whether you realize it or not. Create an awareness, right now, to really listen to the voice. Pay attention to what you hear. What are you saying to yourself? Are your silent words encouraging or discouraging? If they are discouraging, you have developed a bad habit, and it must be eliminated.

The first thing you must do to change a habit of speaking negatively to yourself is to catch yourself doing it.

Since my early days as a speaker, I have included something in every talk about controlling how we think. In *Mind, Time and Passion* I always teach that what we tell ourselves becomes our truth. I've heard Zig say many times,

"Keep telling yourself that often enough and you'll believe it."

Our inner voice, whether we use it consciously or unconsciously, is so powerful that it actually shapes our reality. Guided, that voice has the ability to help us self-correct and self-direct.

I studied Maltz's book very carefully because I realized that my thinking up until then had been accidental, simply a result of my environment. The desire to succeed was burning bright in me. Excited about my new position in management, I was field training agents. I was trying to understand success – for myself, but especially for the people I had committed to help. I felt responsible for leading them in how to think like successful people do. I began to realize that much of our thought patterns and habits are learned in our youth. If our environment wasn't filled with successful people, we may not have been exposed to strategies for controlling thought or dealing with adversity. I learned from *Psycho-Cybernetics* that our subconscious mind (our thoughts) steer our life. We can direct it toward what we want, or, by not understanding the way the mechanism works, cause it to move us in the wrong direction. With our conscious mind, we must carefully choose what we place in our subconscious so that the negative is not allowed to flourish.

George Matthew Adams was a syndicated columnist in Michigan back in the '20s and '30s. He had some profound thoughts about success. He wrote:

"Learn to keep the door shut. Keep out of your mind and out of your world, every element that seeks admittance with no definite helpful end in view."

Are you able to shut out the negative thoughts? This isn't something most people figure out for themselves. First, one must learn that it is possible. From there, the real work begins. It takes diligence to root out every bit of negativity, but the habit built in doing so will change everything.

Almost everyone wishes for a better life. It is the single common denominator we share. But to get a better life, one must get rid of negative thinking, and most people are completely unaware of its effect on them. This is the major reason so many fail. They don't know how to keep the negative out of their world. They think, "I wish I could do that, but I can't."

How many times in a day do you tell yourself "I can't"? How often do you hear it from those around you? To be successful, you need to change that message. You need to purposefully control what you are saying to your subconscious mind. Success begins with telling yourself positive messages. Even if you don't believe it at first, you will eventually believe it. But only if you form the habit of keeping negative self-talk out and allowing only positive self-talk to enter your mind.

So how do you do that? There is only one way. And when I tell you what it is, you may not even believe me. It sounds too easy. But it takes vigilance to apply it. Here is what you need to do: when you hear the negative, replace it with the positive – and then overwhelm your mind with positive.

Let me explain. If you catch yourself saying, "I can't," stop yourself and say, "I can. I can. I can." You must outweigh the negative with positive. Don't brush this off as something "too simple." It may be simple, but it is not easy to change a lifelong habit. It takes continued effort to build a consistently positive state of mind that will direct your activities. Begin today to recognize the very moment that a negative thought enters your mind and take action immediately to root it out!

I recall a salesman who enrolled in a self-improvement program. He was instructed to begin each day in front of the mirror saying, "I am and I can!" over and over. The next morning, his wife had never seen him so excited as he shouted his affirmation. He didn't make it to work that day!

Negative messages are everywhere in our environment. Television and newspapers sensationalize tragedies and disasters. Think of the last time you saw a crowd gathered around the TV in a public place in rapt attention. Unless it was a sporting event, I will bet it was negative – a school shooting, a tornado tearing apart a town, a train derailed, or a murder trial. This is what modern human beings seem to be drawn into. Perhaps it's always been like this. When the guillotine was scheduled in the neighborhood, people in medieval times hurried to stand in the front row. Our technological developments allow us to be saturated with negative information from around the globe. We get up-to-the-minute coverage of every tragic event under the guise of "we must know what is happening". Do we really need to know every negative thing that is occurring worldwide? Resist! Keep the door shut! Turn off the 24/7 news channel, and restrict access to your mind. Allow only the positive to enter.

Never worry

Another common "negative" that people allow to infect their self-talk is worry. I believe one of the reasons so many Americans suffer from depression is that they have formed a habit of worrying. Worry is actually negative self-talk. It is the nagging voice in our heads reminding us of all the things that might go wrong. It eats away our peace of mind.

We worry about people we love and people we dislike. We worry about our children's grades and marriages. We worry about our financial future. If we really listen to ourselves, we'll hear negative statements rattling on and on about things that haven't even happened!

What a colossal waste of time. Why are we worrying about things we cannot control? And if we are worrying about things we <u>can</u> control, then why don't we just do something about them instead?

Zig has often said to me,

"I never worry. That's God's job."

I love when he says that though, frankly, I rather doubt that God spends any time at all worrying! It surely doesn't seem like an activity for the omnipotent, does it?

Decide today that you aren't going to worry anymore either. It is simply a bad habit you developed over time; and like any habit, it is completely possible to eliminate it, as long as you make a persistent effort to do so. Whenever you catch yourself worrying, tell yourself, "I never worry." Then overwhelm your mind with positive statements, saying things like, "I control what I can control. Whatever happens – happens in my best interest. I am strong enough to handle whatever happens."

Stop worrying! It doesn't accomplish anything positive. If you are wrestling with a problem, state it in a positive manner and think on it, pray on it, and decide your course of action. But worrying shouldn't be part of the action plan.

Read chapter one of The Book of Genesis. Anyone who grew up in the faith of Judaism or Christianity will find the text familiar. Perhaps you missed the tie-in to the way you – as a child of God – create your world. It is the same mechanism used by God in creation. Pay attention as you will read "God said" over and over throughout this chapter. It was the spoken Word of God that brought the universe into existence. The WORD is powerful. Never underestimate the power of it. It brought the Son of God to dwell among us.

"...and the Word became flesh."
John 1:14

Words are shaping your life now, too. Surround yourself with people who say positive words. Speak positive thoughts aloud. Control your thinking. Lift up your heart. Choose to be one of the people for whom everything is good. Encourage others as you wish to be encouraged by them. And be vigilant about letting anything negative cross the threshold of your mind. Recognize that you are responsible for your own self-talk. Choose what you will listen to.

Change your life.

Application

Write down the names of the four most positive people you know.

How can you be more like them?

How much news/television is enough? Is that out of control for you? What are you committed to doing about that?

Write three positive affirmations right here that you will commit to saying whenever you need to overwhelm the negative with positive.

What do you waste time worrying about?

What will you tell yourself the next time you begin to worry?

What could you add to your life that would help you to direct your thoughts and form a habit of positive thinking?

Chapter Six

The Power of Positive Thanking

A wealthy man wanted to raise his son with an appreciation for his good fortune. Hoping to teach him gratitude, they went to the country, spending a few nights visiting a family who lived on a rustic farm, barely scraping by. On the way home, the father asked the boy what he had learned. The son said, "I saw that we have one dog, but they have four, and about a dozen cats. We have a pool, but they have a huge creek with rocks and fish. We have imported lanterns to light our patio, but they have stars all the way to the horizon. We have servants, but they serve others. Father, I thank you for showing me how poor we are!"

No matter our economic standing we can carry a grateful heart into the world. It will shape our lives in powerful ways, influencing everything and everyone around us.

Zig Ziglar says it this way:

"Gratitude is the greatest gift God ever gave us."

This was one-on-one lesson that Zig gave me, and I believe this message of gratitude most clearly expresses the way he lives and loves.

For over thirty years, I was the instigator of our conversations. I called every year or couple years, but in the last five years, I've called much more often. My calls now are to "give back" to

Zig – and to thank him for all the years I counted on him to provide the right words of insight when I needed it. My ol' mentor never lets me down. He keeps reminding me and teaching me and inspiring me – even though it is my intention in calling him now to honor him! Funny how that works.

I've noticed how expressing gratitude has five major benefits.

I. Gratitude can smooth the path

Gratitude is attractive. It draws people to you. When we express thankfulness continuously we have a positive outlook on life. Instead of seeing adversity as a something that holds us back, we decide to look upon it as a lesson or a gift – though we may not understand its value right away. We choose to live with the realization that in all things we are to be joyful.

Paul wrote his letter to the Ephesians in the first century and it is timeless. Chapter 5, verse 20 says:

"...giving thanks always, for everything."

No qualifiers. Always. For everything.

When things go wrong, as they frequently do, maintaining an attitude of gratitude is essential. For the last forty years, I have spent a lot of time in airports watching beleaguered gate agents get bullied by frustrated passengers. I've found that magic often happens when I put on a smile and say, "Thanks for working so hard for all of us." Sometimes the magic is simply a smile that spreads from him or her to the next passenger. Other times, that gate agent has done amazing things to help make my journey better! I've had upgraded hotel rooms, free food and beverages, and first-class upgrades – all because I expressed gratitude for someone's effort and recognized the challenges they were facing. I have found that people want to help me when I am grateful to them.

II. *Gratitude can bring us peace*

I was driving recently from Columbus to my home outside of Detroit. It was a beautiful summer afternoon and the traffic was humming along when it began to slow down with no obvious explanation. Ahead of me stretched a line of stationary cars. There was no turn-off, no turn-around, and no end in sight. I stopped myself from slamming my hand against the steering wheel and took a deep breath. I decided to put on some relaxing music, and consciously released the tension in my neck and shoulders.

Within twenty minutes, the line began to move, and after another thirty minutes, the reason for the delay became clear. A car was lying upside down on the road, blocking both lanes. Police and medical help arrived, and as I crept past, I saw a young woman clutching two young children tearfully as two burly men used the "jaws of life" to extricate a trapped passenger from the overturned car. My heart contracted with the pain these poor people were suffering, and I said a prayer for them. I added, "Thank you, Lord, for my safety, and for all that I take for granted."

I could have spent that unexpected hour feeling angry that I was delayed. I could have let all the negative energy create tension and frustration. None of that would have gotten me home sooner, and all of it would have damaged my soul; when in fact, I was the lucky one who arrived home without suffering the trauma of a car accident.

It's easy to take health for granted when we are healthy. It's easy to take people we love for granted when they are not involved in a crisis. That is the opposite of living a grateful life.

111

Instead, live with an awareness that so much is good in our world. This attracts friendships and projects happiness in spite of the stresses and problems of daily life. It allows us to maintain perspective. That perspective can bring us peace in situations of turmoil, calming ourselves and those around us. Reach for the peace that comes from living with a grateful heart.

III. Gratitude unites us with others

Gratitude helps us deepen our relationships with others. For many years, my clients have known they can count on me to help them in any way that I can. I always feel so glad to be chosen to speak at their events and will often suggest other ways I can help them as long as I am there. I've been known to waive my fees to speak at fundraisers they hold for charity. I've stopped in their satellite offices to encourage their management team. I've sat countless times with their agents who needed extra help – whether personally or professionally. On the speaking circuit, that is one uniqueness that I have – and it's paid off in helping my business grow. I honestly believe my clients know they are more than "just clients" to me. They are my friends. Beyond that, it's made my life better and my joy more complete.

How does that apply to your situation? Who in your life can you show your gratitude to by going the "extra mile?" By delivering more than they expect and by genuinely caring about people, you are living a grateful life. The reward is a deepening of relationships that give you a sense of peace and fulfillment. Too many people define friendship as someone with whom they have a long lasting bond and see frequently. What if you modified that definition to include everyone – from the teller at the bank to the lady pushing her grocery cart in your direction? It has always amazed me to hear stories of perfect strangers who endure a tragic event and help one another through it. Hurricane or tornado or bombing victims offer refuge, hope, encouragement, and often act heroically to save one another. Yet, when there is no tragedy to unite them, people pass one another without a glance or even a kind thought. Your life will change when you begin to see everyone through the lens of gratitude. We are all in this together – and none of us get out of here alive!

IV. Gratitude means multiplying our gifts

My church has recently been engaged in a stewardship campaign. Now, if you're normal, the first thing you thought when you read that is that we are hard at work trying to get people to give more money. But that's not what I'm talking about at all! I've begun to learn what it means to be a steward, and the core principle of stewardship is gratitude.

We are called to be stewards, or caretakers, of all that God has given to us, from the earth to our homes to the people in our lives....up to and including our own bodies. A steward sees that everything is a gift from God, and responds with gratitude. In thanks, we are to utilize these gifts by multiplying them.

You probably know the parable of the "good steward." Found in Matthew 25:14 - 30, Jesus tells the story of an owner who is going on a journey. Before his departure, he summons his servants and gives them each a sum of money. In fear, one buries his coins so that he can return it to his master without risking its loss. The other two servants invest, one more successfully than the other. Upon his return, the master praises the servant who invested most wisely, naming him "my good and faithful servant."

We are all given talents and gifts. Some of us choose to bury them, in fear of embarrassment or reprisal. Others use their gifts, but could do so much more. And then there is the "good and faithful servant" who takes the bestowed gifts to the max. This is the person who understands that everyone and everything is a gift, not owned but loaned, given only for this lifetime, to be valued and then multiplied.

How do we multiply our gifts? By sharing them. Those blessed with a great singing voice can choose to sing alone in the shower, or to bring joy to a group – whether on a stage or in a nursing home. Those blessed with mathematical ability can balance only their own checkbook, or they can share this talent as an accountant for a local charity, elderly neighbor, or as a teacher or tutor. We multiply our gifts by bringing gratitude to bear in all our dealings with one another and living with a joyful heart.

V. Gratitude gives us peace

When is enough enough? Is the objective of our lives to keep buying more and having more and getting more? Or is it something deeper than that?

Can we come to a point of just "settling in", and accepting that enough is enough? When that happens, there is a sense of peace and security that comes upon us. We can stop striving to live large, then larger. I experienced this lesson first-hand.

There was a point in my life when I couldn't have enough. I recall boasting that my master bedroom closet was the same size as the master bedroom in our former home. I spent a part of my life surrounded by 4500 square feet, yet it wasn't enough. I had a boat but I wanted to own two boats and two wave runners. My large yard wasn't enough; I needed to be surrounded by acres. I was always working to "get more" and

114

"have more." And that kept me from feeling secure and living in gratitude. It made me feel like a hamster on the wheel in the cage. No matter how fast my little feet turned that wheel, I discovered that I still had further to run and I was still in the cage.

What is really important? Isn't the peace that comes from living a grateful life more important than all the "things" we want to acquire? Possessions are temporal. Our lives are about so much more than that. Decide what is really important to you. Then tell yourself when "enough is enough" and start enjoying the peace that comes from getting off that wheel of dissatisfaction.

If you're going to make some improvements, there are some simple ways to implement gratitude into your daily life.

Expression

Say thank you a lot. As simple as that sounds, most Americans don't say "thank you" very often. Over the last few years, even cashiers have stopped saying it. Instead, as they hand you the receipt for your purchases, they say, "Here you go!" What is that about? When I hear that, I want to meet the manager because a simple but powerful training piece is missing. Any consumer who chooses to spend their money there – when so many choices abound – are owed a simple thank you.

Do you know anyone that never says "thank you"? It's almost as though they expect whatever you just did for them or gave to them. It almost hurts when they take the compliment or the gift, then act as though they don't really care. As though they expected something from you, and ho-hum, this is it. Next. Those hurt feelings make the people around them feel "less," when it's so easy to build them up instead.

Express gratitude. It makes others feel good. And then they smile. And that smile causes endorphins to flood their mind with pleasant feelings. It's scientific. If we have the ability to create those pleasant feelings in other people, how can we not do so? Particularly with the people we care about and live and work amongst, we should take advantage of our ability to make them feel good. It certainly makes our own life easier to be surrounded by happy people!

"Thank you" isn't the only phrase we can use. We can form sentences to communicate what we usually leave unsaid. Like, "You always time the food so that it arrives on the table while it's hot. I'm so grateful!" Or "I like the way you put your personality into that last song you played/danced/sang" or "Whenever I walk in the door, you greet me with a smile. I love that about coming here." Even, "It's so nice spending time with you – even if we are just doing chores together."

Those kinds of statements go a long way to create peaceful relationships. And I've found that the more often you make them, the more often you are led to make them. You may even find those around you doing the same thing!

Honor them

I have been to Zig's home office several times. While his "Wall of Gratitude" has been featured in his books, I will always remember seeing it for the first time. Framed on the wall are 26 photos of the people he credits for building his character and his talents. From his mother to his first-grade teacher to his first employer, Zig honors them by framing their photograph and telling their story to anyone who asks. He also encourages others to list and to recognize the mentors that helped them along the way.

I always try to thank him for taking an interest in me and for guiding me over these last forty years. One day I asked Zig, "What can I do to thank you for everything you've done for me?" His answer rocked my world. He said, "You honor me already by your performance." I have to tell you, that just made me want to pour myself out all the more to my audiences. It's become one of the ways I consciously repay him for his gift of friendship and advice.

Did you ever have the opportunity to see Zig Ziglar at the pinnacle of his career? He had a sketch he did with a working pump, right on the stage. He would be pumping that pump handle and talking a mile a minute. Just thinking about it now makes me smile. There was a time back in 1998 when I'd hired him to speak at my Master Sales Academy. He was on the stage pumping that pump and trying to pound his message into every heart and mind, when his hand slipped. He had cut his finger! Did that stop Zig? Nope. He kept talking while he pulled a handkerchief from his pocket and wrapped it around the finger that was bleeding profusely. He never missed a beat, pumping furiously all the while. What a master! That he sees my platform skills as a payment for his mentorship is so gracious. It makes me feel so grateful.

When my team of trainers accompanied me to take Zig and Jean to lunch, we shared a conversation about gratitude. At the conclusion, one of my trainers asked him, "How can we honor Floyd for all he's done for us?" Zig said, "Honor him by carrying on his legacy". What a perfect circle that creates. This is the eloquence of the mentor/mentee relationship at its finest. We pay back and we pay forward. And by paying forward, we are repaying and honoring those who shaped our lives.

Pay it forward

This phrase became part of the American lexicon with the popularity of a movie, in the year 2000, with the same name, "Pay It Forward". It is the story of a seventh grade boy whose teacher challenges his class to put a plan into action that will change the world. The concept is that the recipient of a favor does not pay the favor back, but instead grants a favor to someone else, who then pays it forward to another – thus affecting the lives of many.

When we live with a grateful heart, we watch for opportunities to bless someone with a pay it forward action. Our local radio station has designated one week each month to this. They broadcast stories sent by participants on the air, and invite others to get involved. They are encouraging an action that several of my students have been doing for years. When you go through a drive-through, pay your own check and that of the person behind you. My students, who are salespeople, attach a business card and handwrite on the back "Have a great day!" The radio station challenges its listeners to do the same thing, calling it "The Drive-through Difference". They report that often the recipient of this blessing will pass it forward by paying for the order of the car behind them!

A wonderful group of my students from Ohio have made a tradition of paying it forward. They put out the word that they are looking for a past graduate who most needs to be re-charged and re-committed to their business. Perhaps it's someone who has been discouraged or had a family obstacle in recent months. They take up a collection to pay that person's admittance to one of my semi-annual FORUMs. They arrange for a hotel room, a food allowance, and even work out a carpool for their transportation. Most often, they insist that the donation be made anonymously. Following the event, they

118

take great joy in watching the "change" in the recipient's business and attitude.

Paying it forward is a terrific way to "give back" in thanksgiving for the blessings we receive.

Thoughtfulness

In this age of technology, it's easy to write a quick e-mail or post an update on Facebook that says "thank you to everyone who wished me a happy birthday". That's good. But there is another way to express gratitude that will make a bigger impact and feel more sincere. What if you actually handwrote a note? With a pen, and on paper. (Wow....when is the last time you did that?)

There is something so personal about selecting the card or stationery, then, in your own unique handwriting, crafting a message meant for only one person to read. It is the ultimate compliment, and well worth the time it takes to look up the address and actually find a stamp.

We can express gratitude over the phone, too. We spend hours and hours on our cell phones. If you are in business, you call with an objective, and while you may spend a few moments schmoozing, the conversation was clearly intended to be a business call. Sometimes, because that's our frame of reference, we allow it to bleed into our personal lives as well. We call people we know and love, spend a moment connecting, and then get right down to it – discussing the agenda we had organized in our minds before we dialed.

What if you called to say "hello" without an agenda? After your initial greeting, what if you asked questions that led to conversation – during which you primarily listened? A simple telephone call can be an incredible way to express gratitude.

Forgive

The president of my company, Mike Pallin, often quotes his spiritual director who teaches, "Forgive everyone everything, all of the time." What a challenge that is! How can we forgive those who don't ask for forgiveness or express remorse? Forgive EVERYthing? Really? No matter what?

Yet, what is the alternative? When we are hurt, we cover the pain with anger. Like a drop of dye in a pool of water – it colors everything. Nurturing hurt feelings stifles joy and creativity. It prevents us from living to the fullest. So, how can we get past the anger and pain – especially when it is justified? Forgiveness.

One of my favorite illustrations of this profound spiritual principle comes from the life of a young woman who suffered greatly at the hands of her neighbors and friends. They viciously killed every member of her family, some as she watched, with machetes and hatchets. As you read this, you are probably thinking it is an "old story" – perhaps of an incident that occurred several centuries ago. But it is a new story.

The uprising of the Hutu against their neighbors, the Tutsi, happened in 1994. Neighbor rose against neighbor, and were swept into a churning wave of depravity and evil that destroyed the lives of over 800,000 during the 91-day Rwandan Holocaust.

Immaculee Ilibagiza, a 22-year-old college student who was visiting her family over the holiday when the genocide began, survived three months of terror and starvation by hiding in a tiny bathroom with 21 other women. If you have not read *Left To Tell*, don't miss it. Years later, she was given an opportunity to meet face-to-face with her brother's murderer, the same man who hunted for her during the siege. The guards expected and supported retaliation appropriate to his crimes. Instead, Immaculee stunned them by offering her forgiveness.

How could that happen? It is only with grace. Grace comes from allowing God to be in charge. It is a gift we receive when we turn our lives over to Him. Instead of the human tendency to forgive only those who ask for forgiveness, the Bible tells story after story of God's forgiveness being given before it is even requested.

This is not an easy thing to do. My father never asked for my forgiveness. He never said he loved me, or even talked to me much – other than to yell at me. Of course, I was raised in the era before Oprah and "Parent Magazine"; so hopefully, fathers are better informed these days. We had a difficult relationship, my dad and I. He spent over thirty years being depressed, angry, and resentful because he had nothing.

In spite of that, he imprinted characteristics within me that have shaped my life, and for which I am grateful. Maybe the best lesson he ever gave me was that when you say you're going to do something, you do it. That's even become part of my Core Values, and is recited daily by thousands of my students. It came from my father, and I am grateful to him. I have forgiven him for his shortcomings, and am grateful for the gifts of character that he gave to me.

We are told to "give thanks unceasingly" and have "hearts filled with gratitude". Such beautiful commands, but so difficult to do because gratitude cannot exist unless there is forgiveness first. Why is this so challenging for us? Because other people are in the mix. Human beings are generally difficult to live with and get along with, and they frequently let us down. (Have you noticed?) We may love them, but it's hard to love every one of them unconditionally and unceasingly. That's why forgiveness is so important.

What about forgiving the people who are ungrateful or who don't "deserve" to be forgiven? They haven't even acknowledged their shortcomings, yet we are to forgive them? Yes. Forgiveness is a gift we give to ourselves when we give it to others. It is a healing balm for anger, hurt, and disappointment. Forgiveness is the prerequisite for living in gratitude.

The gift of attention

At Chuck Colson's memorial service, his daughter, Emily, spoke of his accomplishments. He had served in President Nixon's cabinet, working many long hours in service to our country, sacrificing family time and relationships. His involvement in Watergate resulted in a prison sentence, which changed everything for him. Dedicating the remainder of his life to prison ministry, Colson still kept a very strenuous schedule. Yet when his daughter telephoned him or visited with her autistic son, Max, Chuck was completely engaged. He gave them both undivided attention.

During the eulogy, Emily explained how her father was totally present for them, and, she discovered, for every member of the family. Because of her age, she had seen how he'd parented "before" his conversion and could compare it to the way he parented "afterward." He put God first and family second, ahead of everything else that was going on around him.

Does it take a prison sentence to gain that perspective? I don't think so. I think we need to ask ourselves a few questions, and allow the answers to illuminate the truth for each of us.

Who are the important people in your life today?

Are you fully present to them when they are speaking?

Are you completely engaged in their lives?

What would they say during your eulogy?

It's time to stop making excuses and lying to ourselves. No matter how full our lives are, we are not too busy to give undivided attention. We have time to do better, *if we so desire*. Give those you love the gift of your attention, and then accept whatever they give back to you with joy.

Gifting

Woodworking is my favorite hobby. I can while away a couple hours just strolling through a wood specialty shop. Making useful items brings me so much pleasure. Recently I made a pair of Adirondack chairs to use in the back yard. They've consumed many hours, yet there's something therapeutic about seeing the effort materialize into a real product.

One of my early projects taught me a great lesson. I wanted to make a jewelry box for my sister, Denise. I spent hours dreaming up the right plan. I selected wood with perfect and beautiful grain. I worked hard to get every detail just right. Though I usually had a tendency to rush the finishing steps, I took my time doing the fine sanding and layering of shellac. I wanted that box to be perfect.

It hid in its pretty Christmas wrap under the tree while I waited with impatient anticipation for her to open it. Then the moment arrived. She liked it. She smiled and said that she did, and she said "thank you," and then she set it aside. I was crushed! I spent all that time to perfect every detail, and she just set it aside! That jewelry box taught me a powerful lesson about gratitude.

There wasn't a chance in the world that Denise could have responded in a way that would have satisfied me. I realized that I had been expecting her to praise me to the high heavens, and I learned that when I make and give a gift, I have to do it for me. I have to bask in the enjoyment of the creating and of the giving, and not expect abundant thanks. The praise I give myself has to be enough.

You cannot force someone to be grateful, and unmet expectations only lead to disappointment, negating the whole idea of gifting. Whether the gift is something we make, a place or idea we share, or just simple, undivided attention, allow it to be given with no strings attached.

Open your heart to gratitude

Most people just don't live with a grateful heart. They are constantly striving for "more" instead of living in a state of thankfulness. If you need a bit of perspective, spend an hour in the cancer ward at your local children's hospital. Look into the eyes of the mothers holding a sick toddler on their lap – hoping against hope that this is the day they will hear good news. What problems did you mention you had? I bet they pale in comparison to the ones faced by those who are sitting in that waiting room.

Keep your perspective! You have so much to be grateful for – yet you tend to forget that truth! Remind yourself right now. Remind yourself of all the blessings that have been poured down upon you over the last decades. Thank God for your health, for your family, for your friends, for your passions and your gifts. Thank Him for the food and shelter that are unknown to millions on this very day, but which we so often take for granted. Be grateful. Be thankful. Be aware of the blessings to which you've grown accustomed. Stop taking so much for granted.

From this moment forward, determine that you will live with a grateful heart.

Application

What are you most grateful for?

Who would go on your own "Wall of Gratitude"?

Who needs your forgiveness? When can you meet with (or speak with) that person so that you can express or ask for forgiveness?

Who has let you down? In spite of that, was there a gift that you were given by them?

What are your greatest talents/gifts?

What idea for sharing your talents did you have while you were reading this chapter (even if it seemed silly)?

Who needs you to give them your undivided attention? How will you do that?

How do you wish to be described at your eulogy?

Chapter Seven

It's What You Do....

What causes a person to succeed? It's not who you are. It's what you DO that makes you a success. And what you do is determined by your character.

Take a good look at yourself in the mirror. Who do you see? No doubt, the experiences you've had have shaped your life. But more important than the experiences themselves is your response to them. Let me ask you this: What kind of character do you have? Are you a person of integrity?

Webster's dictionary describes "character" as "one of the attributes or features that make up and distinguish an individual." You may notice that there is no modifier that says character is "good" or "bad." It's all character. Let's add that modifier. What if you decided to strive for a higher degree of "good character"? If you knew you could be shaped into a better version of yourself, would you be willing?

While improving your interior is a life-long journey, one way to take a big step forward is by allowing integrity to permeate every facet of your life.

Coaches say that natural talent only gets a person so far. Becoming better at anything takes humility. It takes a willingness to learn, to be teachable. Sports coaches look for players with ability, of course. But when building a team, they strive to find those who are willing to learn, who can let go of the "old way" and try new things. They look for players that are adaptable. While you may not be trying out for a team, that adaptability is the key to making deep personal change, as well. Open your mind right now and commit that you are willing to grow and change.

Your character impacts everything and everyone. It broadcasts loud and clear all around you, in every situation. What is it saying? Does it say, "This is a person of integrity"?

My mentor and friend, Zig Ziglar, puts it this way:

"Integrity is the most important ingredient."

Integrity is more than the way a person acts in one circumstance. It is the collection of behaviors that reflect one's inner core values. It is a consistent series of choices. It is a way of living that is directed by a set of basic beliefs that are held throughout every life experience. Integrity guides decisions, stamps out regret, and unites people in long-term relationships – bringing peace. It is the place where what is on the inside enters the world. It is where words and actions meet.

This isn't as complicated as it may sound. I recall attending a national convention as a young man. Perusing the array of workshop choices, I recall one title that caught my attention. The seminar was called, "The 23 Characteristics of Success". I immediately rejected the possibility of attending it. If success really required all of those qualities, I was in a heap of trouble!

So, let's keep it simple. True integrity is really a combination of two characteristics that, when woven together, form the character of successful people.

1. Self-control

Self-control is the willingness to adhere to a set of decisions you have made in advance.

If you raised children, you know that even the simplest of tasks can be difficult for a child to accomplish without direct supervision. They need to be reminded again and again before they develop the self-control to manage their behavior in spite of temptations to take short cuts or skip the activity all together.

In our western culture we brush our children's first teeth before bedtime and again after breakfast until the child is deemed old enough to do the brushing on their own. Despite this, many often forgo the routine. It would come as no surprise to any parent the actual number of kids in middle school that have not brushed their teeth for several days! They have not yet made the transition between knowing what they are supposed to do and actually doing it consistently on their own.

Self-control means removing the emotional response or option from the equation. We don't do or not do based on how we "feel," but rather, our actions are chosen in advance, and then carried out, despite the way we feel in the moment.

My friend, Cavett Robert, was the founder of The National Speakers Association. A remarkable man of integrity, he defined character as:

"The ability to carry out a good resolution long after the excitement of the moment has passed."

If one must continually decide a course of action in the moment, we are likely to take the easy way out, make mistakes or miss opportunities. This is why self-control is such an essential component of integrity. Character with integrity means that we have made a decision based on our values, then we take the action that is directed by those values. It's the reason we pick up our socks or eat green leafy vegetables or complete the tasks to which we committed, even when it's not convenient. Our self-control allows us to ignore the impulse to cut corners or do "what feels good" in the moment. We live in integrity.

We have all worked with people that lack the conviction to follow through with their commitments. Seeing the "easy way out" swayed them. Some make excuses that justify their diversion. "No one will ever know," "it doesn't really matter anyway," "it's too difficult," or "no one else cares." It takes the habit of intentionally living in integrity to overcome the powerful siren song calling us to neglect our obligations and commitments.

On the job

In most hiring situations talent and experience win the job. Not so when I am selecting associates. Throughout my career, I have always hired for character. Talent can be developed with observation, study and practice. A person with a strong sense of integrity is a willing learner and will work hard to learn what they need to succeed. They will also work harder and longer than those who have never developed that integrity. Instead of finding faults in others or relying on everything they already know, they labor to apply new knowledge. A person with good character is great to have around, and I take pleasure in discovering their strengths.

If I find them unsuited for the job for which they were hired, I can often find another place in the company for them – sometimes creating a unique position that will showcase their best assets. When I discover someone with depth of character, I want that person to stay in my company and in my life.

Surrounding ourselves with people of integrity makes all of us better. The people in my company are honorable,; they do what they say they will do, as do my friends. What can you do in your life and in your business that will draw those of integrity into your environment?

My oldest son, Floyd Junior, holds two jobs. In addition to his full-time career, he has managed my company's shipping department for the last twenty-five years. He always delivers. Whatever he may lack in business savvy, he makes up for one hundred times over because of his integrity. He always does what he says he will do. He believes he can do it. He may make forty unsuccessful attempts, or have to drive for hours, or stay up all night, but if he said he'd deliver something by tomorrow morning, I can count on him to do so. He won't quit until he has done what he promised.

That willingness to live up to your commitment, to complete the task, is a vital sign on integrity.

My father had it, too. He was the best milkman that Twin Pines ever had. Twice he built the biggest, most prosperous routes by delivering superior service and asking for referrals. I spent many Saturday mornings with him in the milk truck. He insisted that every milk bottle line up perfectly, with the Twin Pines logo facing the street. Though as a kid I hated it, he would make me run back to adjust them if they didn't meet his standards.

Dad knocked on doors, too. He asked for referrals and built a successful business because he always did what he said he would do. He held himself to a high standard - to never make a mistake on a delivery. He had a whole host of flaws – he swore, smoked cigarettes, gambled, and grumbled – all of them a lot! But he taught me one of the most important principles of integrity there is – do what you say you will do, sometimes more, just never less. The foundation of integrity is self-control. This means to resist caving in to the temptation to deliver less than you promised. A person of integrity makes a decision about their behavior or belief and then sticks to it, no matter what.

2. *Acting in line with your convictions*

When we live with integrity, it means we live in line with our values. What we do and say on the "outside" matches what we believe and hold dear on the "inside." An old friend of mine always said, "Talk is cheap." What a true statement! It's not always easy to behave in a way that reflects our values. In fact, sometimes the "easy route" is in direct violation of what we hold dear.

I recall a student who earned a six-figure income selling timeshares. Windy was making the transition to residential real estate and ended up in my class. One day she confided that while she had supported her family with a comfortable lifestyle, she had never felt good about her former profession because it was so clear in her mind that the decision she had to ask people to make was not really in their best interests. She loved my class because she finally had permission to act in line with her inner values. She had an opportunity to help people make good decisions, that they would thank her for later.

Internal conflict can eat at a person, causing unhappiness and stress. The only way to resolve that angst is to step up and say "no more" – even if doing so is costly. The choices made by Martin Luther King, Jr. exemplify this. We revere him for having the fortitude to act upon his convictions, even when it meant placing his beloved wife and children in harm's way. If your actions, though in line with your values, threatened those you love, would you persist?

Another example of acting with integrity is Irena Sendler. Though she has been nominated, she has not yet won a Nobel Peace Prize. Do you know her story?

A member of the Polish Underground, Irena posed as a plumber's assistant in the Warsaw ghetto during World War II. She hid babies in the bottom of her toolbox, smuggling them out to those who would care for them. She took 2500 infants and small children right past the German officers and their dogs at the gate, saving them from the fate of their parents – the Nazi gas chambers. Captured, she was tortured and sentenced to death. Sendler survived the war to find the jars she and her associates had buried which contained a list of the children's names. She spent many years attempting to reunite them with the survivors in their families. Irena Sendler lived with integrity. She was a hero for saving lives, but the core of her actions was her unwillingness to ignore a great injustice. She knew the Nazis were starving and persecuting those of Jewish descent. So she did what she could do. She didn't save adults, though I imagine she wished that were possible. She could save children, their parents' hope for the future. She took action. She did what she could do. That is integrity.

All of us grew up with stories of heroes – from those who ran the underground railroad more than a century ago, to the men and women who battled inequities in their workplaces and neighborhoods during the last fifty years, to those willing to sacrifice their lives on a terrorist-high-jacked plane. These are people whose actions stand for what is right even when faced with a lack of popularity or imminent death. They had the courage to act in line with their convictions, willing to sacrifice their safety rather than violate their beliefs and principles. Their stories exemplify integrity.

Every one of us is called to live a life with integrity. It is not just for the "heroes" among us, nor does this only apply on occasions when life hangs in the balance. We set the example for one another in our daily lives, by our ordinary conduct in every circumstance. Our actions bespeak the truth of our inner beliefs. Do people hold you in high regard? Are they jusitifed in trusting your word? If you say you will do something, do you follow through, no matter what?

Remember the Pharisees at the time of Jesus? They were powerful men, established leaders of their faith and known for their zealous willingness to uphold every one of 613 mitzvoth (commandments) set forth in the Torah. They were perfect on the outside. But their hearts were not in line with their actions. Jesus called them hypocrites. His words are a challenge to us some two thousand years later. He calls us to integrity from the inside out when he says,

"Hypocrites, well did Isaiah prophesy about you when he said: This people honors me with their lips, but their hearts are far from me."
Matthew 15: 7-8

Integrity is when our actions and words meet with our inner belief. This is what living in line with our convictions really means. Hypocrisy is not about making mistakes or falling short, it is about pretending to be someone on the outside that does not match with who you are on the inside.

For over fifty years, Zig Ziglar has had impeccable integrity. He wouldn't so much as have a cup of coffee alone with a woman, concerned that it might give someone cause to question his intentions. His daily conduct has always been in line with his values: God first, then family; even when that created difficulty. Each of us must determine our inner values, and then live by them. It is so much more than being concerned with what others may think of us, it's about knowing within our own mind's eye the truth about who we really are.

I love the example Reuben Gonzolas set for all of us. Entered in the Racquetball Hall Of Fame in 2000, he was once ranked the number one racquetball player in the world. But his career got off to a rather shaky start. On match point of the final match during his very first professional tournament, the referee called Gonzolas' final shot "in." Stopping the game, Rueben explained that his shot had actually hit the wall first, before it hit the floor. The serve went to his opponent, who then won the match.

Asked to explain why he disqualified himself as the winner when the line judge had determined the ball "fair," Gonzolas explained, "It was the only thing I could do to maintain my integrity."

Something like this had never happened before at a tournament. Gonzolas was willing to risk it all for the sake of his integrity. Are you? Are you willing to be honest, no matter what the cost?

I often quote my mother, who always said, "Sometimes you can believe a thief, but you can never believe a liar." There were certainly times in my childhood that I told a lie to avoid getting in trouble or hurting someone. Since adulthood, however, I have been determined to be honest – no matter the personal cost. I frequently say, "I'll always tell you like it is." Of course, sometimes the truth is good to hear, and sometimes it's not. But the important thing is that truth be told regardless of the outcome.

I am reminded of the king who needed an heir to whom to pass his throne. He decided to choose a boy from the kingdom who could become a great ruler, so he initiated a competition. Hundreds of young men rose to the challenge. For months, they were tested for prowess at academics, strength, endurance and swordsmanship.

When the field had narrowed to the ten most extraordinary boys, the king offered one last test to determine his heir. He gave each child a single seed of corn, saying that since the kingdom was heavily dependent on agriculture, a great leader must be skilled at cultivation. Three weeks later, each boy stood before the king with his little pot holding a small plant of corn.

As the king examined each one, he said, "Is this what you grew from the seed I gave you?"

When he reached the final boy, he found himself looking at a barren pot of soil. "Is this what you grew from the seed I gave you?" Expecting punishment for being the only one to have failed to cultivate even a hint of living plant, the boy sorrowfully nodded his affirmation.

With great joy and ceremony, the king lifted the boy to the crowd and proclaimed, "This is the boy that shall become my son. He alone exhibits the greatest characteristic of leadership – integrity."

To everyone's surprise, the king had given each boy a boiled seed, which could never sprout. Despite the temptation to switch seeds and win the kingdom, this child exhibited royal integrity.

Zig told me many times that although teaching my students selling skills was important, I must...

"... never forget to work on building their character, too, because if one or the other is missing their success will be short-lived."

A person of good character lives up to their predetermined standards, despite temptations to lower them.

Adversity can be a real test of character. I can recall a few people that I thought had integrity, but whose actions betrayed a lack thereof when money was involved. Money tends to bring out the worst in some folks. It can make people behave selfishly. It can woo the desperate into revealing their true colors. It's easy to honor high-minded principles when times are good, but pressure often reveals the truth. True integrity is facing adversity with honor and truth. True integrity is what you do when no one is watching; it is how you treat others when there is nothing to gain.

Integrity is highlighted as a critical character trait of godly people. The Apostle Paul tells Titus,

"In everything set them an example by doing what is good. In your teaching show integrity, seriousness and soundness of speech that cannot be condemned, so that those who oppose you may be ashamed because they have nothing bad to say about us."
Titus 2: 7-8

Of course, Paul was concerned about the behavior of Titus as a representative of the new church. Similarly, our own actions reflect on our companies, our profession, our families, and ourselves.

Having seven grandchildren, I can tell you firsthand that kids watch everything we do. They recognize when our actions conflict with what we "said" was right. They remember how we handle occasions when the rules of honesty and integrity are violated.

Many a parent has reached the shopping center parking lot to discover their preschooler has secreted an unpaid item within their pocket. How we help them manage its return (or not) forms the building blocks that impact decisions they make for the rest of their lives.

In the Old Testament, Proverbs 1:3 says,

"Receive instruction in wise dealing and the discipline of wise thoughtfulness, righteousness, justice, and integrity."

A thirst for justice and a life of integrity provide the foundation of the Paul Schneider story. A minister in Germany, when Nazi leadership required he weave his Christian message into a patriotic embrace of Hitler's message, he refused. Feeling they were not living in line with Christian values, he was also unwilling to give communion to the powerful Nazi leaders in his congregation. These actions led to his internment at the Birkenholtz concentration camp. There, when the German national anthem was played for the prisoners, Schneider refused to remove his cap.

He lived his life for justice. In line with his values, he rejected the possibility of acting outside of his integrity, and for that he suffered torture and death. Paul Schneider became a martyr for the sake of his beliefs. While it is unlikely that any one of us will be called upon to make a life or death decision by our actions, we can be inspired by those who have. This depth of integrity calls us to live in line with what is right and just – and motivates us to stand up for what we hold dear.

How to raise your integrity level

There are three things you can do to deepen your integrity.

1. Awareness

The first is the easiest, and you have already begun. It is that *awareness* we talked about in the first chapter. You are newly aware of your integrity level, and wish to elevate it, to become the highest and best person you can possibly be. Because of that awareness, you will think about your daily choices and what they indicate. Suddenly, you will find examples appearing in your world – at home and at work – of both high and low levels of integrity. You will observe others making choices that both impress and disgust you. Embrace that awareness. It is the first key to change.

2. *Communicate*

The second thing you can do to deepen your integrity is to talk about it with others. Share your thoughts, ask questions, and pose hypotheticals.

There is a woman whom I have always admired. She is kind and warm. She sacrifices for her family, cares for her aging parents, and encourages those around her. A few weeks ago, she told me excitedly about an experience she had at the supermarket. It seems that when the butcher weighed her roast, he punched in the wrong number for the cost per pound. She triumphantly left the store having paid only $3.75 for a four pound standing rib roast.

I listened to this story in dismay. She was completely oblivious to the lack of character her behavior revealed. She expected me to celebrate her good fortune, and I had no choice but to share my disappointment instead.

A similar incident occurred when my son was young. He came back from a trip to a soda machine triumphantly holding a can of Coca Cola AND the quarters he had deposited into the dispenser. In addition to receiving the can, the quarters had spit out of the change-release and he was ecstatic that he had gotten the soda for free. A direct march to the front desk of the hotel gave us a few minutes to talk about what is "right." He agreed that taking something that belongs to someone else – even if they are unaware and nameless - is not just.

This is not simply a question of honesty. It is instead a deeper issue of justice and of integrity. Do our actions model our inner beliefs? The small ways we make choices can often reveal where we are flawed (or not) in our larger choices as well. When we lament the character of politicians or mourn the tattered fabric of good 'ol American values, are we pointing fingers in the wrong direction? Zig has always said, "When you have one finger pointing at the problem, there are three others pointing at the cause." How is it possible for America to be steeped in good character if the majority of her citizens are wallowing in a low level of integrity?

3. *Choose your friends*

Third, choose to surround yourself with people of integrity. Like attracts like. What kind of character do the people you associate with demonstrate? When I consider my friends, I am struck with how well I have chosen. Each one of them does what they say they will do, and exhibits wise choices when they act. They care about others, and are true both in their conversation and in their actions. When adversity strikes, they bear it with grace and humility, instead of grumbling. They are successful at their businesses, but more than that, they are successful at their lives. They desire to do the right thing in every situation, and they challenge me to be a better me.

My friends are also good listeners. They exude empathy and try to really listen. They are actively and compassionately engaged in conversation – rather than taking things at face value or forcing their opinion upon another. Instead, they seek to understand the meaning behind the words of one another, and contribute to the resolution of a challenge. They believe in a positive outcome before there is any evidence to support such a belief.

One of my students was suffering from a lack of results. I called him to encourage him and left him with a few things to do and to think about. Two weeks later, everything had turned around for him. His entire attitude was changed, and the results followed that transformation. He said, "Floyd told me to 'Let go, and let God.' I have been repeating that as a mantra in every situation that used to worry me, and I've changed my response to adversity."

Who do you spend your time with? Are you keeping connections with people that drag you downward? Eliminate the toxic people from your life, and focus on building relationships with people that live the way you want to live. Choose to associate with those who lift you up and encourage you.

Making a change

It sounds simple, yet embracing these three actions – self-control, acting in line with your convictions and choosing your friends - will lead you to a new level of character, imbued with integrity.

Application

What experiences have you had that tested your integrity?

If you were in those situations now, how would you respond?

Who is in your life that you regard as an example of high integrity? Why?

Who is in your life that should be weeded out?

On a scale of 1 to 10, rate your own integrity/character.

What is something you have trouble doing once you promise to do it?

Chapter Eight

How To Get What You Want

What is it that you want? A happy marriage? Good health? Obedient children? A fulfilling career? Money? Can you see beyond the next year and into the future? Are you thinking of short-term or long-term goals? Too many folks in America have set a goal to simply make it to the next paycheck. And so they do. What if you set your sights higher than that?

Some time ago, I began sharing a poem with my audiences to inspire them to think big:

I bargained with Life for a penny,
And Life would pay no more,
However I begged at evening
When I counted my scanty store;

For Life is a just employer,
He gives you what you ask,
But once you have set the wages,
Why, you must bear the task.

I worked for a menial's hire,
Only to learn, dismayed,
That any wage I had asked of Life,
Life would have gladly paid.

J.B. Rittenhouse

Have you been bargaining with life? Have you settled for less than you should? I am reminded of John Brown who comes to our annual events. He sat in the classroom, set an income goal and hit it. The following year, he set a higher income goal and hit it. Finally, the third year, he began asking himself why he had set his first two goals so low.

I am assuming that if you are reading this book, you have within you the desire to reach out for more than you currently have – more peace, more wealth, more....what? If you read the first chapter carefully, you know what you want. We spent time together working on the difference between a goal and a fantasy, and if you completed the assignment at the end of Chapter One, you have a real goal – something you want for you.

But knowing what you want is only the first half of the equation. Most people find the second half a bit more difficult: helping others to get what they want.

Helping others get what they want

As a new real estate salesman, I heard Zig Ziglar's message before I ever met the man. Those were the days of lp records (for you young folks, that's like a big cd that was played on a phonograph).   Since the time Zig started in the training business, his core message was about helping other people get what they want.   For me, those words changed my entire perspective about selling. According to the old saying, "Selling is simple: Find out what people want and show them how to get it." That's classic Zig.   Suddenly, sitting at a kitchen table with a potential client was more than just "qualifying."   I began to think in terms of finding a problem and offering a solution.   That kind of thinking would shape the future of training in real estate.

In fact, it even won me a car! Late one evening I was sitting in a lounge when a fireman walked in. He went around the room asking everyone, "Would you like to buy a ticket to the Detroit Fireman's Field Day?" I had a new awareness of giving to others, and as I bought a ticket, I felt that desire bubble to the surface. I knew just what he could say that would help him get what he most wanted. I said, "Could I give you a tip that would help you sell more tickets?" With his permission, I suggested that instead of asking them to buy one ticket he could say, "Do you have children? How many?" And then peel off one for each kid.   He replied, "That's a great idea! By the way, how many kids do you have?" He peeled off two more tickets which, chuckling, I bought. It was the third ticket he sold me that won the car. It was awarded on the field of a Detroit Tigers game and while the car was wonderful, its message in my life was more profound: When I put others first and help them get what they want, I can have anything I desire.

Zig says it this way:

"You can have everything in life you want if you will just help enough other people get what they want."

This is not a new concept. Two thousand years ago Luke included it in his gospel. See chapter 6, verse 38, and you'll find this:

"Give, and it will be given to you: good measure, pressed down, shaken together, and running over, will be given to you. For with the same measure you measure it will be measured back to you."

Read that verse again. Read "...the same measure you measure..." and think about the scale you use to measure your own generosity. Have you been expecting to receive more than that measure which you use to give?

Do you know what happens when you give? You get to be a *giver*. It's my mother, Gertrude, who planted the first seeds of that lesson in me. My brother, Kenneth, supported his drug habit by stealing everything my folks had. My parents, who never had a lot anyway, found themselves with even less. He stole the radio, the television, and my father's wallet. They learned pretty quickly not to replace the stolen items, lest the replacements be stolen, too.

A lesson from Mom

About eight months into my new sales career, I was penniless and feeling hopeless. Have you ever felt that way? I needed somewhere to go – but almost anywhere I could go would either cost money or increase the pressure under which I was already reeling. There was only one place I could get a free cup of coffee and an understanding ear... to my parents' home.

Sitting at the dining room table, it all started tumbling out. I confided to my mother the situation I was in – how hard I was working, how much pressure I felt to succeed, how much my wife and boys were counting on me. And I began to cry.

Before long, my mother stood up and walked to the dresser, which sat along one wall of the dining room. She used her hip to nudge it aside, revealing a hole my father had cut into the wall. Mom reached inside to pull out the purse she'd concealed from my brother. Taking out a few dollars – which was almost all of what she had – she insisted that I accept the money as a gift, rather than a loan. I remember her saying, "Son, sometimes when a man has a few dollars in his pocket, he just feels better about himself." She was right. Those few dollars not only gave me hope, they became a turning point for me. They and the spirit in which they were given - along with the message I'd heard from Zig - inspired me to begin practicing the "Get By Giving" philosophy.

It wasn't easy at first.

I was on my way to the next appointment and zooming down the highway. On the side of the road was a car with its hood up, children hanging out the windows, and a distressed-looking lady behind the wheel. As I passed I thought to myself, "She needs help!" Preoccupied, and focused on myself, I didn't stop. Yet, somehow the farther I got from her, the worse I felt. I kept

148

thinking about those dollars my mother had given to me. I thought about how being a giver was a way of life I had never really tried out. The more I thought and the farther I went, the feeling that I was missing an opportunity to help someone in need bothered me more and more. Several miles down the road, I made a u turn and changed direction. The woman was still there when I reached her 20 minutes later. She still needed my help. She and the kids piled into my car and I drove them to a gas station to fill her gas can. It was so satisfying to help her get that car back on the road that it wasn't until both cars were underway again, the kids waving goodbye as they passed, that I realized I had completely forgotten to tell her I was in real estate and to give her my card! Not exactly the right way to grow my fledging business, was it?

Yet within just a few days, it came back to me. For the first time in almost a year, I received an incoming call for business. Then another. And another. Was this a coincidence? I don't think so. I believe these events were linked together by my change in attitude. That u turn was more than just a physical turning of my car around. It was a u turn in the way I had been thinking up until then. For my whole life, I had thought about my needs and myself first. As soon as I started putting other people first I was rewarded with unexpected, unrelated blessings. It was only the beginning of the way I've lived my life ever since then. For decades now I have believed that there is a spiritual law, a law of the universe, that is as profound and guaranteed as the law of gravity. It goes like this: *We Get By Giving*.

I'm certainly not the first person to discover this incredible truth. Like most great lessons, it began with an awareness that was reinforced when I took action. I needed to apply the law by putting it to work in my life before I could reap the benefits of it, and claim it as my own truth.

Get By Giving

The Platinum Rule is a book written by my friend and fellow speaker, Art Fettig. In it, he says that if we only give because we want to receive, we are simply trading.

It's when we give because we <u>have</u> that we get something back that is better than an even exchange.

Floyd Wickman Courses was my first company. We put its corporate philosophy everywhere the company name appeared. It said, "We Get By Giving". There was a time in my career when I honestly believe that any client, if asked, would have said that I would do anything for them. (It was true, I would have!) As I lived by the principle of giving my time, my money, and my energy without expectation of repayment, I discovered that the best way to give was to do so in secret. Though I always tried to do it discretely and without fanfare, my trainers often told one another stories of times they saw me giving. My actions set an example for them, and they also became givers. As a result, I have had an extraordinary life surrounded by like-minded individuals who treat our clients with the "Get By Giving" philosophy. It has become much more than just a company slogan; it is our way of life.

When I sold Floyd Wickman Courses and created a new company, I expanded the philosophy to a full set of Core Values that could be shared and used to help us make decisions. Now, whenever there is an issue to resolve, the Core Values direct us to make the right decision. We have printed them on a huge banner that hangs on the front wall of every meeting room we use. We open our corporate meetings by reciting them aloud. We live and breathe them, and expect one another to do the same.

Core Values

At the outset of every training program we teach, we present them to our students. We explain the practical advantages of living by a set of Core Values that is nearly counter-cultural. Then we tell our students that if they wish to participate in the training program, we would like them to agree to live by these same principles. We teach them what each phrase means with stories and illustrations, and show them how to put their power to work. At the end of each session we all stand to recite our Core Values aloud. The room resounds with strident voices asserting their commitment, as we pound on the table to emphasize each phrase. Our Core Values are:

To always....

...Live by the "Get By Giving" philosophy

...Make my client's number one goal, my number one goal

...Live up to my standards despite temptation to lower them

...Be willing to work toward the common good

…Do what I say I will do, sometimes more, just never less.

If you receive a business card from one of our past graduates, you'll find that often they've printed these Core Values on the back of the card. Frequently, our students use them as part of their signature line when sending e-mails. Most important, it's a way of holding ourselves to a higher standard, reminding ourselves of our beliefs, and spreading the word – inspiring others to live in the same way.

What would our world be like if everyone lived by this set of Core Values? Customer service would reach unsurpassed heights. Charities and foundations would find endless supplies of volunteers. Mentors would help those in need reach their goals. Businesses and families would find relationships more satisfying.

Give when you can

What happens to us when we don't live by the Get By Giving philosophy? Missed opportunities can teach us profound lessons, too. As a professional speaker, I've flown over eight million miles. That's a lot of time spent in airports! But I'll never forget the opportunity I missed that taught me to act upon my impulse to give.

The last flight of the day from Seattle to Detroit was boarding and I was tired. Finally, I'd be on the plane and headed home. In the days before electronic ticketing, a paper ticket was the only way to board a flight, and could only be gotten outside security at the front counter. A young man rushed up to the gate agent and explained in anguish that he'd lost his paper ticket. The gate agent told him he'd have to go to the front

152

counter to replace it, but that in doing so, he'd certainly miss the flight. He pleaded for her help to make the flight. His family was counting on his arrival in Detroit. I listened sympathetically to his predicament, and then boarded the plane – knowing he'd be unable to make his destination.

After the plane was in the air, the drama of that young man's dilemma sunk my spirits lower and lower. Why hadn't I given him my ticket? Why hadn't I just turned over my credit card to purchase him a ticket right there? Why had I done nothing to solve his problem, when certainly, I had the power to do so? The further I flew, the worse I felt.

Though I never saw the young man again, he helped me to learn a powerful lesson about giving: we have a responsibility to give when we can. NOT giving can actually cause us pain. I learned that the farther you get from the opportunity you missed, the worse you feel. And I made a commitment to myself: never again would I fail to act when I could help someone.

Perhaps you've seen homeless beggars at the intersections of your highways holding signs that say, "Hungry" or "Lost job. Please help." Perhaps you, like many of us, have averted your eyes and hoped that the light would turn green quickly so you didn't have to look at them and feel guilty. Maybe you've even given to them – only to be ridiculed by the passenger in your car.

Retired Archbishop Harry Flynn tells a story about one such incident. It was a cold winter evening when he rolled down his window to pass money to a man that was begging at the stoplight. His passenger, a student at the university, said, "Why did you give him money? Didn't you notice that he was wearing $100 boots on his feet? Clearly, he is not what he appears to be!" To which Archbishop Flynn replied, "If I get to the heaven tonight and am laughed at for being so foolish to give to that man, I would be much happier than if I get to heaven and have to explain how I could see a man who was hungry ask for my help only to be denied."

He was in a unique position to know this truth. His life had been steeped in the "giving" philosophy from his early thirties. I recall a story he often told about meeting a woman who had snuck her cat onto a train. The cat was hiding under the seat beyond her reach and she asked Flynn's help to extricate him.

"Is he de-clawed?"

"No."

"Does he bite?"

"Not usually."

Reluctantly, the young priest crawled onto the floor and carefully placed the cat into its carrier. This act of giving, with no expectation of receiving anything in return, began a friendship that was kept alive for years through Christmas cards and letters. Upon her death, the woman bequeathed one million dollars to the seminary that Flynn was currently serving.

Do you live by the "Get By Giving" philosophy? Have you made a commitment to yourself that you will act immediately to help others without judgment or an expectation of repayment? Are you prepared to receive the blessings that are promised to those who give without expecting compensation?

Application

Will you agree to live by each of the five Core Values?

Are there any that should be added or modified to fit your work/family experience?

Post your Core Values somewhere that you can see them daily.

Commit to reading them aloud with enthusiasm each day.

Use them to guide you as you make decisions.

Chapter Nine

Moving Forward

Anyone who has read this book from the beginning and done the Applications following each chapter has demonstrated the strength to embark on the journey to gain or regain success.

It's not the willingness to "start" we need to talk about now. You've done that. Now we must ensure that you persevere. I wish I could tell you that it will be smooth sailing until you reach your destination, but I cannot. It takes tremendous fortitude to reach a goal, because once it is set, it is subject to a whole host of thoughts and experiences that will cause you to question its practicality and likelihood. Feeling discouragement and defeat is all too common. In spite of these emotions, you must let nothing prevent you from achieving your objective. You must control your thinking to move forward.

Soon after Linda and I stopped trying to retire and I made the commitment to begin a new company, the doubts set in. I clearly recall heading home from the hardware store when anxiety struck. Quickly, I pulled into a nearby parking lot – the church we had just joined – and took some deep breaths. I was using my affirmations, trying to envision my rebirth, yet I felt discouragement and hopelessness crowd right into the car with me. I dialed Zig. Thank God for this life-long mentor who always answers my calls! I'll never forget what he said that day. He said,

"How can you be a 'has-been' when the best is yet to come?"

That afternoon, I thought he meant that when I die, I will have an eternity of happiness and fulfillment in heaven. While that is a comforting thought, it wasn't at all what Zig wanted me to understand.

His goal was to assure me that right now, at this point in my life, I had the "best" part of life ahead of me! It took me several weeks of pondering his message to grasp that. Yet, time and time again, I have seen the same force at work in the lives of those around me. It is true for you, too.

The blessing

Gary Sisson was the second trainer to join my company. Having had a career as a pharmacist, he had a terrific memory and was smart as a whip. He also had a successful real estate career under his belt. Gary was the kind of guy who could sell ice cubes to Eskimos. Like me, however, he operated within a set of Core Values so if he didn't honestly believe you needed something, he would never consider convincing you to buy it.

In 2004, this wonderful trainer who was such an asset to my company had a stroke. After the first rush of concern, we learned that he would live. It wasn't until much later that we learned how difficult the transition from "before" to "after" would be for him.

When Gary woke up in the hospital his beloved wife, Lauren, was there. Since his vision was impaired and he couldn't remember much more than his name, they spent two days crying. They mourned the loss of his career. They fretted over how they would make ends meet. Gary cried, "My whole life is over!"

On the third day, they made a decision to move forward. They looked at one another and said, "We have to be thankful for what we have. And this is what we've got."

Together, they began to walk the halls of the hospital with purpose. Lauren would ask him, "What do you remember?" and they would review the basics that Gary needed to recollect.

Then the test results came in. It was bad news. The post-stroke MRI had revealed an aneurism in Gary's brain. He would have to undergo a life-threatening surgery to remove it or risk instantaneous death upon its rupture. Within another week, the surgery was a success and the long road to recovery began.

They simplified their lives by selling their home. Lauren landed a secure job with her father several states away. They enrolled their young daughter in a new school there, and eventually Gary found work selling granite countertops. He jokes that it's a quicker sale and the customers don't expect him to remember their names for more than an afternoon! The new job doesn't require the kind of travel that being a trainer did, so Gary has had a chance to see Olivia play every tennis game for several seasons. It's a different lifestyle, but he's having fun. He keeps the home fires burning while Lauren works, and he has never stopped feeling grateful for the stroke. You see, the aneurism had been there for a while, so Gary will tell you "the stroke saved my life."

The Sissons built a whole new life around the basics: God, family, and gratitude. They decided to control their thinking and move forward.

Remember the trapeze artist analogy? While an acrobat is swinging on one trapeze, it's comfortable and safe. To catch the next trapeze involves a bit of risk. You cannot catch the second trapeze without letting go of the first one or you'll tear your arms off.

So, too, must you be willing to let go of "where you are" in order to get "where you wish to be."

Even when the place you land isn't comfortable, you must let go of the "old" and work the "new" until it becomes comfortable. All of life is like that. Why would success be any different?

"For God did not give us the spirit of timidity, but the spirit of power, of love and of self-discipline."
Second Timothy 1:7

When you're feeling beat up or wrestling with fear, remember that God made us tougher than we think! By controlling our thoughts and choosing to persevere instead of giving up, we take control of our destination. We chart the course to our goal.

More from Gary

I know the secret to "keeping it going" when we feel overwhelmed. It's probably best told by my ol' friend, Gary, though, so I will resume his story. A few years after his challenges with the stroke, he found himself in great pain. His knees were giving out! Love and self-encouragement got him through the tough times he faced yet again. It is these traits that blend together to form the characteristic of persistence.

Gary had both knees replaced. Then the right knee became infected, so to achieve his goal of walking without pain he endured a second surgery and a total of eight months in rehab. Through it all, he told himself,

"Just get to the stick."

Once he remembered why that phrase was important – and that took a while! – he made it his mission to inspire others in the rehab center, telling and retelling the story I'd shared with him many years before.

Persistence

I was speaking to a general audience of about 1500 people. Since most of my speeches are given to Realtors, it's a bit unusual to have someone who is truly elderly in the room. But there he was in front of me, and my eyes were continually drawn to the dignified gentleman in the third row who frequently nodded his agreement with what I was saying about persistence. After the speech, he waited until everyone else had left the room, then approached me. He said, "You seem to be a collector of stories, Floyd, and I think I have one you may be interested in hearing."

I had been speaking that day about overcoming adversity and drawing the strength to be persistent, even when it seems like the odds are stacked against you. He took a deep breath and began.

"My grandparents were slaves who picked cotton. Each morning, the overseer would line them up and they would look out upon the acres and acres they were expected to clear before the sun set. A daunting task, to say the least! Once they began, the eldest worker would pick up a stick and throw it out into the cotton field. As someone expressed discouragement or began to tire, they would say to one another, "Just get to the stick."

Sometimes only whispered in desperation by an individual who knew that to stop would bring a painful beating or even death, that phrase would be repeated all through the day.

Of course, upon reaching the stick, someone would pick it up and toss it again further ahead into the field. In this way, my people were able to make a near-impossible task become possible."

I have spent a lot of time over the years thinking about those that suffered in the cotton fields of our country. Imagine with me the generations of families who toiled under the hot sun, doing back- and spirit-breaking work while fearing for their lives – and realize that it only ended in the last century. Indeed, it is almost impossible to comprehend.

What an incredible life-lesson in perspective and persistence I was given that day. I am so grateful for the dear man who took the time to share it with me. I believe he would be pleased with how many lives he has inspired through my trainers and me as we have shared his family's story.

When challenges seem too difficult to bear, tell yourself, "Just get to the stick."

That phrase is how Gary managed to maintain optimism throughout the months he suffered during the reconstruction of his knees. He would set the date for the next surgery and tell himself, "Just get to the stick." Of course, after the surgery, he threw that stick to "walk well enough to go home," and then, "heal enough to drive." By breaking our goals into attainable steps and setting dates to accomplish those steps, we can achieve almost anything that at first seems nearly impossible. This is the stuff of persistence.

Self-stoppers

Everyone has heard of someone who is defined as a self-starter. Rarely does anyone acknowledge himself or herself as a self-stopper, however. Whether acknowledged or not, stopping ourselves from achieving our goals is much more common. Once we determine that we want to achieve something or do something, it can be difficult to keep at it when the going gets tough. People fail not because they were unwilling to start, but because they quit too soon. We must prevent ourselves from stopping before we reach the goal. This is especially difficult because every person faces challenges on the way to greatness.

Linda and I worked with a fitness coach who often spoke about his professional frustration. He would take on a new client, clearly identify a set of goals, and then devise a plan for achieving them. He would get the client's agreement and commitment. But often within a few weeks the client would stop coming in! He said, "The hardest thing to do is to keep someone motivated before they see results." I think that applies to all of us.

We live in an age of instant gratification. We eat fast food, peruse 100+ channels on our big screen TVs, and accelerate our cars through yellow lights. You and I don't like waiting for anything – from lines at the checkout counter to the loading time of a YouTube video. We expect to achieve our goals and objectives quickly and efficiently, too. That's why this chapter is so important.

Isaiah 40:31 calls to us from before the first century, saying:

"They that wait upon the Lord shall renew their strength."

No question about it, if we are going to accomplish our goals and gain prosperity, we will need strength. The journey is difficult and the course beset with obstacles. We definitely need to have our strength renewed along the way. Think about how you have felt over the last months (or years). Have you felt weak or disheartened? Once the goal is set and we have new energy and drive, those feelings go away for a while. But they will be back, and we will once again need renewal as we progress on our quest for achievement.

So, how do we cash in on the renewal of strength we've been promised? The answer is right there in front of us. We need to "wait upon the Lord."

Frankly, there is really only one time we willingly use the word "wait," and that is when we are telling someone else to do it! You and I are reluctant waiters. We are impatient, preferring to skip the first, basic steps of something and move right on to the "important" ones. Yet, it is when we wait that we regain the strength we need.

The Book of Isaiah was written in Hebrew, of course, so the meaning is a bit different than when translated to the English language. Used as a verb, Qavah ("קוה") means to twist, to stretch, and to endure. Isn't that exactly what we do when we need strength? We twist in discomfort as we battle through weakness. We stretch toward our destination, reaching for greater endurance. When we wait upon the Lord, we suffer through hardship, we persist toward the goal until our strength is renewed and we reach it, finding ourselves comfortable doing what was once very uncomfortable. Our strength is renewed.

Waiting

My study of one of the martial arts, Choi Kwang Do, taught me a profound lesson about waiting and persistence.

I learned early on there were only ten moves to master; however, it took a couple years of attending two sessions a week before all ten were revealed. That was frustrating! I recall waiting for the "good stuff," but at each session we would once again practice the same basic moves.

Our teacher asked us to stand in a certain way. At first I thought, "Oh, man, this is uncomfortable!" He would slap my arm down, or move my foot out to get me into the right position. Yet three weeks later, I found myself standing in the correct form easily, with no adjustments. And the best part is that it felt right.

When the moves become second nature, you are able to link them together with fluidity and grace. The positions actually become a physical memory needing no conscious thought to be executed perfectly. But it takes time for that to happen, and it's difficult to be patient and allow the process to unfold.

This is a powerful lesson that applies to whatever we are trying to learn. It is *always* uncomfortable at the beginning. I usually try to communicate this by saying:

Work it 'til it works.

Are you really at your best? If you are trying hard, but are not at your best – keep working it until it works. Comparing yourself to others can cause you to give up or feel like you'll never achieve what they have done. Stop! Your goal should be to become the best "you," however that form is expressed. Zig says it this way:

"Anything worth doing well is worth doing poorly first."

That can be a difficult lesson to assimilate. Successful in so many areas of our life, we expect to be good at everything else, too. Failing or accomplishing less than we expect is difficult. We have a tendency to say, "I can't" or "That's not for me," or "This isn't going to work," instead of accepting poor performance as the precursor to mastery.

You have already begun the process of self-improvement or you wouldn't be sharing this chapter with me. What you must realize now is that to become the best "you," you will have to continue working at it. Remember that if you do something long enough and hard enough and diligently enough – you will master it. Step by step you will be brought closer to your goal. Even though the steps may be small, as long as you keep moving in the right direction, you will eventually reach your destination.

Michael Jordan is an undisputed basketball legend. He is the holder of thirteen NBA records, most of them for scoring. His long-time coach, Phil Jackson, said that at the start of his career in 1984, he was strong at penetrating but not at shooting from the outside. Jackson made sure Jordan knew his accuracy wasn't up to professional standards, and then watched Jordan put in his gym-time. During the off-season, he made hundreds of shots each day, and while he doesn't rank in the top 50 "all time greats," he has a very respectable 581 successful three-pointers out of 1778 attempts, certainly more than most players in the NBA, and a decent average. Michael said it this way:

"My attitude is that if you push me towards something that you think is a weakness, then I will turn that perceived weakness into a strength."

Turning a weakness into a strength begins with the right attitude. Achievers believe that it is possible to change. That's what I love about them. Instead of relying on their natural ability alone, they think differently. They persevere toward greatness. Those who make it to the top of their professions are unwilling to accept failure. No matter who tells them "no," they persist. They sacrifice the hours and the sweat it takes to reach their goal. Then they set a new one.

This kind of thinking isn't just for athletes. It applies to every walk of life.   The books, *The Spy Who Came In From The Cold*, *The Diary Of Anne Frank*, *Alice In Wonderland* and *Moby Dick* were all rejected many times until their authors found a publisher willing to take their work. Elvis Presley was fired from The Grand Ol' Opry after only one performance. Marilyn Monroe heard a modeling agency say, "Get married. You don't have a future in show business." A studio executive wrote, "Can't sing. Can't act. Balding. Dances a little." about Fred Astaire. Often, the biggest hurdle to overcome on the way to achieving greatness is finding the inner strength to persist in spite of all evidence that one should quit.

Perseverance isn't logical. In fact, often it defies logic.

When we face obstacles, adversities and doubt, we need to remember that God gives us encouragement in His presence and helps us find the strength to persevere.

Inner strength isn't necessarily something we are born with. Instead, it is something that can be developed. When the naysayers discourage us and the goal seems impossible to reach, we have to remember that we are not alone.

Zig Ziglar often encouraged me by saying:

"You + God = Enough"

I am grateful for this lesson because the journey to success can seem pretty lonely. There have been so many times in my life when I felt it was all up to me and only me. Can you relate to that? By putting such pressure on ourselves, we create an environment in which it is difficult to thrive. The seeds of doubt begin to dig their roots into one's best intensions; fear begins to surface.

Adding God to the mix changes our perspective. Eternal, omnipotent and omnipresent, He is beside us and within us. He encourages us with His Word. His Spirit sustains and inspires us.

So we throw the stick. It helps us hit short-term goals and track our progress toward the "big goal" while we take the small steps that will ultimately get us to our destination. We decide to work it until it works, accepting that we may perform poorly until we have mastered the task. Our sustained effort is combined with inspiration because along the way, we partner with our God. We invite Him into our hopes and dreams and rely on His strength so that we are able to continue moving forward.

About Zig Ziglar

Often described as the world's foremost authority on motivation, Zig Ziglar is an American icon. He is the author more than 30 books – ten of which made the best sellers lists. He has spoken all over the world, both live and televised, and has appeared with six U.S. presidents. His "I Can" programs, taught in schools around the country, have improved self-esteem and battled in the war against drugs, impacting the lives of thousands of children.

He is in The National Speakers Hall Of Fame and recognized with The Lifetime Member Award, The Cavett Award, and The Master of Influence Award.

Zig Ziglar's message of empowerment and values has touched millions over the last half-century. For the last forty years, he mentored a man named Floyd Wickman and his legacy and impact have been magnified through that relationship.

The Authors

Floyd Wickman was chosen one of the Top 25 Most Influential People in Real Estate by The National Association of REALTORS and REALTOR Magazine, an honor he received for impacting such a large number of people with his speaking and teaching over the last three decades. As a CPAE (Council of Peers Award of Excellence) he was inducted into The National Speakers Association Hall Of Fame, a lifetime achievement he shares with such legends as Dr. Norman Vincent Peale, Earl Nightingale, Art Linkletter, and Zig Ziglar. More than twenty years ago, Floyd sold his first million audio products and was the recipient of the "Platinum Award." He has given more than 3000 speeches, founded two successful companies, and written seven top-selling books.

Yet, at age 60, he began to wonder if his life's journey was ending. The accomplishments and accolades were in the rearview mirror, and the future looked bleak. A series of one-on-one conversations with his mentor, Zig Ziglar, changed his thinking and created his "re-birth." Floyd was reminded of the lessons he'd learned that made him a success - and found new energy and hope.

Mary Johnson

The legacy of Zig Ziglar, passed to Floyd Wickman, lives on in me. For over thirty years, I have been applying their message of success. They helped me raise three remarkable children and build three profitable businesses. And, I have been happy and peaceful along the journey.

It has been an incredible privilege to immerse myself in the pools of wisdom drawn from the great storehouse of knowledge left to us through Zig and Floyd. I am called now to be the vessel that carries these lessons to you, so that you, too, can have everything you desire from this life.

Sit beside me at the feet of these two great masters of success.

Special Thanks

Thank you to Mike Pallin and Gale Carlos who helped in so many ways – from critiquing to editing, advising, marketing, and especially encouraging over the last four years. Thank you to The Zig Ziglar Foundation and especially to Laurie Magers (and her infamous red pen!). Thanks to Margaret and Joe Rudich and to all who read early copies to improve them. The errors remaining are mine alone!

Thank you to Julie Escobar and Rob Verderber for a million things they did of which I am completely unaware – but without which this book wouldn't have happened. I am filled with gratitude for the magic artistry of Mark Baron. He took the idea of the "Z" in the clouds that Zig's daughter, Julie, saw following her father's death, which so inspired her (read her article in "Guideposts") and made it work on our cover. You're amazing, Mark!

Thank you to our Floyd Wickman Team (especially Steve Linn), to our Master Sales Society FORUM family members who bought advance copies to help us launch, and to all our precious Clients and friends that jumped in to help us hit our goal. Floyd and I are so very grateful to you all.

CPSIA information can be obtained at www.ICGtesting.com
Printed in the USA
BVOW03s2036261213

340259BV00001B/1/P